CONTEXTURES

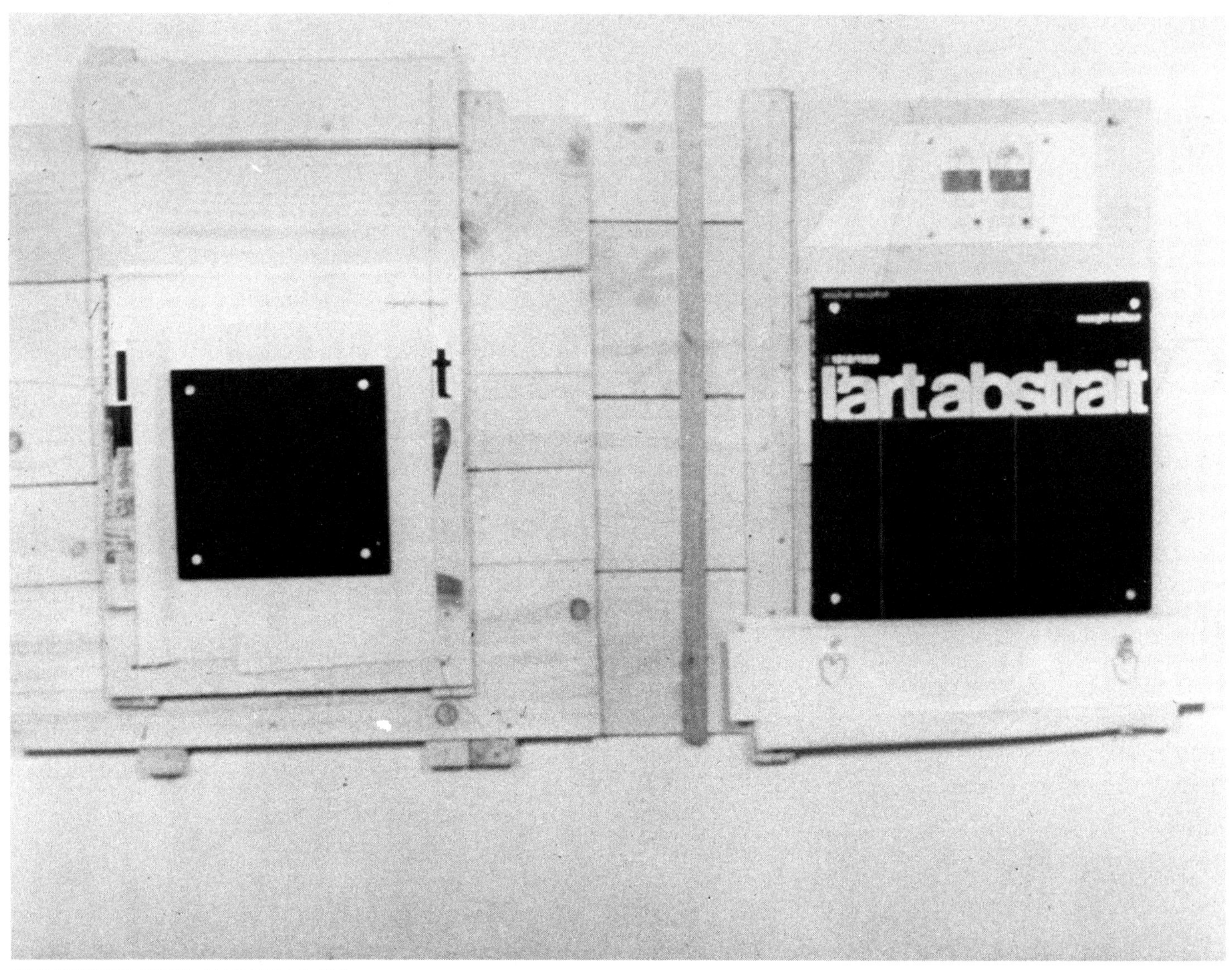

57. RANDY WILLIAMS. *L'Art Abstract. 1977*

CONTEXTURES

by
Linda Goode Bryant
and
Marcy S. Philips

Just Above Midtown, Inc., New York

ACKNOWLEDGMENTS

There are many people who have lent their support and comfort to us throughout this hectic and harried time. Evelyn Philips and Gylbert Coker diligently assisted us in editing the initial manuscript. Randy Williams and Bill Day designed the book with a keen eye toward the impact of the visual with the verbal.

A special thanks should go to the artists who allowed us to interview them, frequently in their studios amidst their work. Their personal observations, often frank and revealing, were invaluable and added immensely to our own insights into the subject. Also, David Kermani of the Tibor de Nagy Gallery, Ellery Kurtz of the Andrew Crispo Gallery and Richard Oosterom of the Terry Dintenfass Gallery were extremely cooperative and provided us with much needed information.

Our appreciation is extended to the Department of Cultural Affairs for the City of New York and The New York State Council on the Arts which provided public funds so that this book could be published.

A special and warm thanks is gratefully extended to our families and friends who were supportive and encouraging to us. They put up with late hours, long dissertations on contemporary art, erratic behavior and the sound of the typewriter well into the night with no complaints.

Warm appreciation is again extended to Randy Williams, whose knowledge and insights helped to formulate the Theory of Contextures.

A co-authorship can present unique, and sometimes difficult, problems so we would finally like to thank each other. We have not only accomplished what we believe to be an important art historical document, but we have also managed to remain good friends throughout the process.

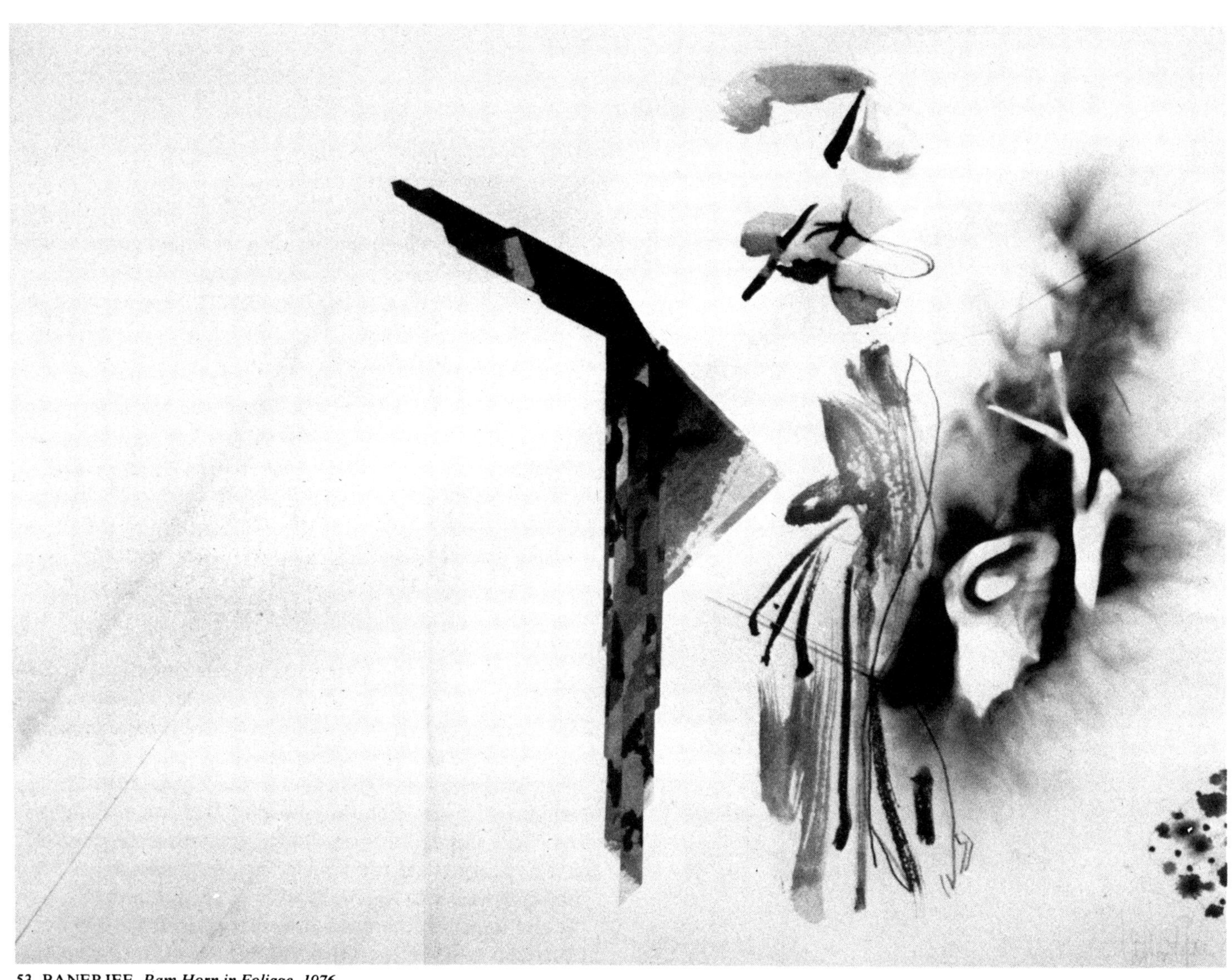

53. BANERJEE. *Ram Horn in Foliage. 1976*

CONTENTS

Acknowledgments	5
Preface	9
Abstract American Art: 1945-1978	11
Contextures	37
Afro-American Artists Working in the Abstract Continuum	79
Color Plates	80
Afterword	98
Notes	101
Bibliography	102
List of Illustrations	104
Index	106
Credits	107

PREFACE

The purpose of this book is two-fold: to provide a stylistic discussion on American abstract art since the mid 1940s, placing Afro-American artists working in this tradition within its context; and to discuss, for the first time, a style that has been developing since the early 1970s which we have termed Contextures. Much of the information was obtained through interviews with the artists.

Our objective in both is to provide the basis on which further research and documentation can occur. Hopefully, a more equitable climate will result in which the public is afforded greater exposure to new, as well as often neglected, artists and their developments.

Linda Goode Bryant
Marcy S. Philips
February, 1978

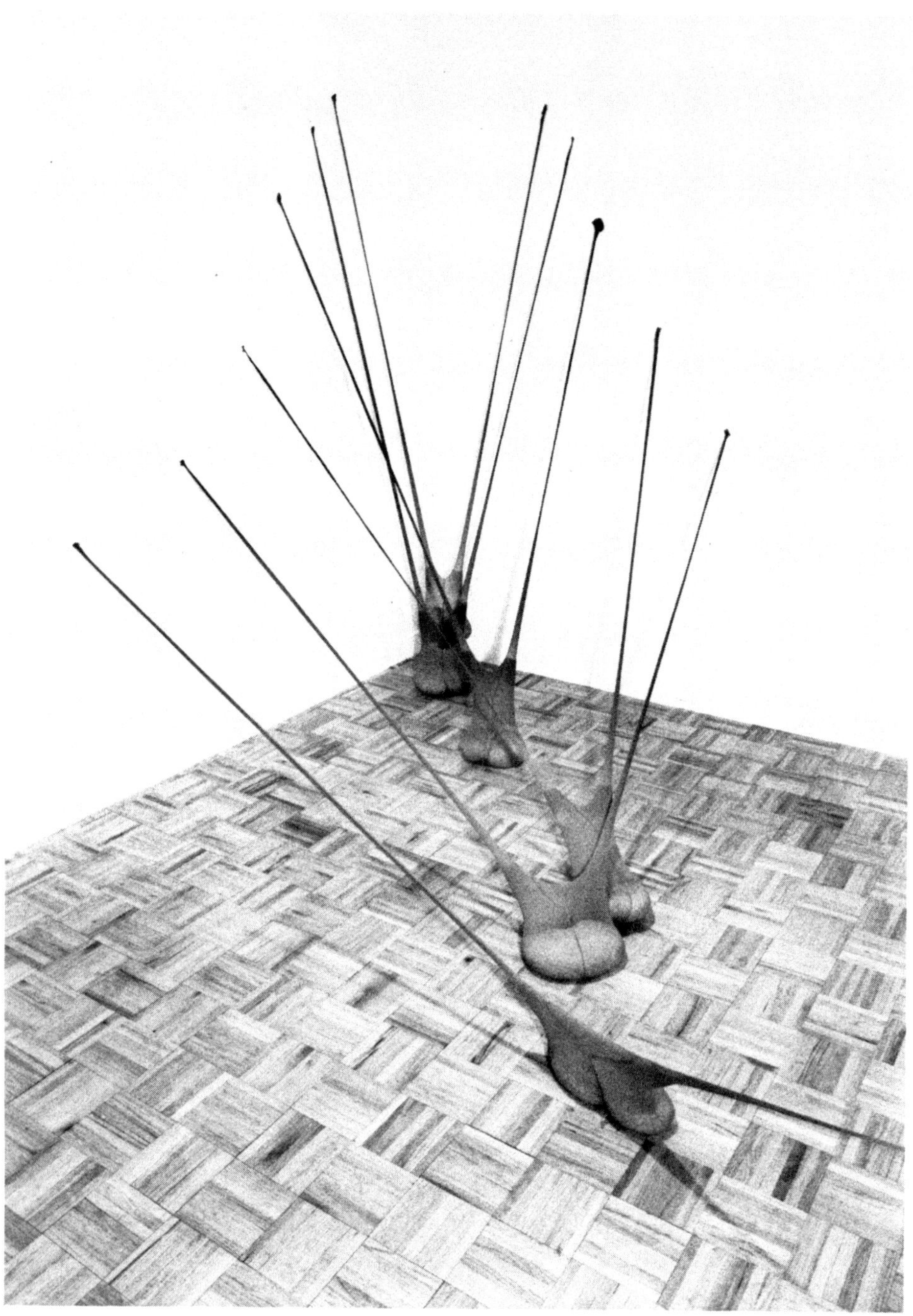

31. SENGA NENGUDI. *I. 1977*

ABSTRACT AMERICAN ART: 1945-1978

A characteristic distinction between styles predating Impressionism and the onset of modern art is the nature and status afforded art and the art object during the Twentieth Century. While a variety of styles has developed during this period, in general, they have virtually all emphasized, exposed and acknowledged the natural and indigenous physical and perceptual properties of art. No longer subordinate, adherent to or dependent directly upon definitions determined and originating outside its own confines, the art object becomes physically and perceptually autonomous, embodying its own characteristics and qualities which in turn define its nature and content.

The artist's process and materials have been primary elements utilized to expose the innate properties of the art object. The degree and extent to which they are used have generally determined the nature of the dichotomy which will exist between the art object and the external object or environ.

Early attitudinal changes which begin to reflect this dichotomy can be noted in the works of the Impressionists during the late Nineteenth Century. The purpose of art to pose as, and essentially be defined by, an external object was exposed to a method of immediacy. This approach illuminated the visual effects of process and the inherent characteristics of materials, namely the physical and perceptual qualities which originated from within the picture frame. The art object began to exhibit its own self-contained qualities, which, as in the works of Cezanne, begin to compete with its external determinants for visual dominance. This tension between the art object and external object increases in the Cubists' works. Disassembled structures, forms and compositional arrangements are emphasized and become the primary factor in determining the perceptual nature and intent of the works. These distorted and disembodied forms, however, can be reconstructed and reassembled to resemble an external object. Therefore they maintain a certain dependency on definition from external determinants.

The confrontation between the art object and the external object becomes more direct in the works of the Dadaists, particularly Duchamp. The two literally become synonymous as the artist eliminates any distinction between them through a method predicated on a philosophy and process of choice. Through transformed, disembodied and distorted forms, the Surrealists further reduce the art's literal dependency on outside physical and perceptual phenomena. The art object becomes the arena in which the metaphysical properties of a given object or experience are interpreted. Through this approach, the visual vocabulary of the artist is expanded as an allegiance to and concern for the rendering of literal images are decreased.

A complete separation between the properties which define the art object and the properties which define an external object primarily occurs in abstract styles since Surrealism. By expanding the structural distortions and the philosophical and aesthetic premises reflected by the Dadaists and Surrealists, the personal experience, intent and objectives of the artist are escalated, and become the content element of the art object. By altering the positions and status of the art object, reality, artist, concept, materials and process, the post-Surrealist styles define their specific philosophical and aesthetic objectives. The process has been exposed to such an extent that it acts as a major determinant in establishing the physical and perceptual properties and qualities which define the art object, as well as the manner in which it will be perceived.

This particular use of process notably begins with the Abstract Expressionists when a complete separation between the physical and perceptual properties of art and those of an external object has been achieved. The elements contained within the picture plane cease to go outside for clarification and definition. They exist in and of themselves determining their own particular reality. The process (in essence a series of spontaneous and systemic movements) determines the nature and content of their works. The artist and nature become one. "I am nature . . . My concern is with the rhythms of nature . . . I work from the inside out like nature."[1] The Abstract Expressionists synthesized the automatism and personal aspects of the Surrealists with the seemingly reactionary aspects of the Dadaists and eliminated the geometric constrictions of the Cubists in order to erase any suggestion of subject matter. It is through this synthesis that the personal feelings of the artists are illuminated and the prior visual premises are expanded.

The philosophical premise of Abstract Expressionism is primarily based on the personal freedom and expression of the artists. Thus, their principles, approach, method and visual presentations will vary distinctly. By allowing themselves the choice to be mobile, gestural and passionate, they create completely abstracted form from their expressive execution. This freedom, therefore, accounts for the apparent visual differences among their works, implying that this movement is based on a historical designation rather than on a stylistic classification in which common and consistent elements exist throughout.

Despite the many dissimilarities inherent in the uniquely personal qualities of their work, the Abstract Expressionists all paint on a large scale. For the most part these paintings have no single point of interest since all areas of the painting are of equal importance. The work is done in an overall pattern, and as the eye is focused on the whole image rather than a partial one, a feeling of totality is achieved. This increase in scale and effect of an all-over pattern makes the canvases seem to extend beyond the boundaries of the frame, surrounding the viewer, and drawing him/her into the work. The visual experience, therefore, becomes a very personal one, as is the creative process for the artist.

Mark Rothko's works in the 1940s arose from the surrealistic fluidity of fanciful images. By the 1950s, as a simplification of color, line and movement evolved, Rothko's paintings took on a mystical tone. Further emphasizing the ethereal quality of the works are the thinly painted, soft-edged rectangles which float on a color field. The viewer is surrounded by the large works and aroused by the richness and directness of the color experience, whether it be the bright luminosity of Rothko's earlier works or the more somber tones evident in his later paintings.

Coming from a Social Realist background, Franz Kline began to reduce color and form in the late 1940s to concentrate on gesture and movement. Kline created strong designs by using a broad house painter's brush which produced wide strokes, and enamel paint which was used because of its glossiness and fluidity. Giant black lines move energetically across the white background, creating images reminiscent of Oriental calligraphy or urban structural designs. The impact, however, is both simplified and immediate.

Progressing from a very detailed realism in the late 1940s to a cubist and futurist mode of expression, Ed Clark moved to Paris in 1952 where he began to paint in an abstract expressionist manner. The manipulation of the medium and the energy of the brush strokes became the reality of Clark's work, rather than the subject matter itself. All reference to nature was eliminated, replaced by a love for paint, and a consuming interest in form and color which are distributed at will around the canvas.

Clark's works in the mid 1950s became so gestural that the strokes could not be contained within the confines of a rectangular canvas. The brush strokes shot outward and upward in a surge of energetic abandon, breaking out of their four-sided frame, forcing themselves upon the viewer.

In the 1960s, Clark began to use his format of the oval and the stripe. The first group of paintings which were actually elliptical in shape exhibited the long, splashy brushwork of his earlier works, and the bristles of the push-broom that Clark used to apply the paint left traces of thin lines that cut horizontally across the canvas. The effect implies a dynamic interplay between rounded canvas, bright color and sharp thrusting forms.

Retaining the ellipse, Clark further developed this approach by floating the shape within an atmospheric color field of a rectangular frame (fig. 1). Later the division between field and ellipse became less distinct. The ovoid shape at times merely acts to break up the horizontals. At other times, this ellipse disappears altogether and the form is only implied.

Since 1970, Ed Clark has begun to use tape to delineate both the stripes and the oval. This procedure resulted in a more regimented and less spontaneous feel to the work. Drawing the ellipse first, Clark then marks off with masking tape the width and placement of the bands. The horizontal flow in the varied thicknesses of the resulting stripes constitutes the linear design. Walking along its horizontal length, Clark pours acrylic paint onto the canvas. He removes the tape just before the paint dries in order to achieve a smooth, pure line. Clark has developed a sense of color and technique which allows him to predict the blendings that will occur while pouring. He maintains a rapport with the process which he sees as a physical, almost sexual, oneness with his work (pl. 1).

Jackson Pollock's expressionistic and individualistic approach to art developed out of and during his participation in the W.P.A. Federal Art Project (1935-43). It was in the late 1940s that Pollock began to move into the more free expression of drop painting. This occurred after his work with Mexican muralist, David Alfaro Siqueiros, who was using spray guns, air brushes and methods which allowed for a spontaneous application of paint.

Placing his canvas on a floor or ground, Pollock gave himself the freedom to move around all four sides or to

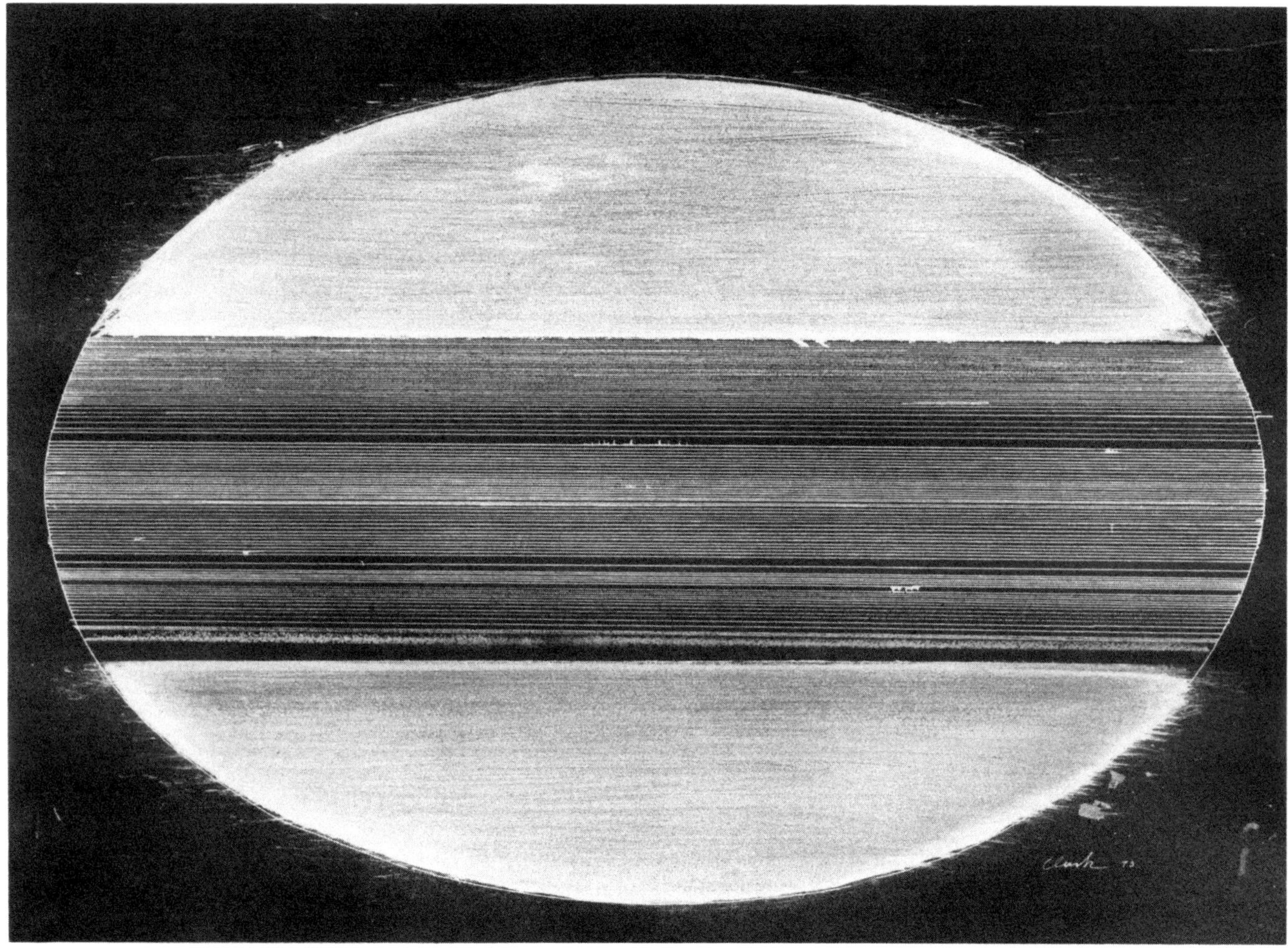

1. ED CLARK. *Black and White Drawing. 1970*

walk on it, allowing himself to be both literally and figuratively in his art. The artist's whole body could participate in the creative process giving his emotional energies a voice in the final product. Pollock also preferred using sticks and knives to drip and drop his paint on the canvas to the traditional use of palettes and brushes. Any accidental or spontaneous splattering and spill that occurred was simply incorporated into the loose structure of the painting. "The registration of the act of creation as a unique and dramatic event, and as an episode in a process of personality, was its main subject matter or concern. All the exhibited marks of freedom in handling and execution, were left in visible evidence in the finished work to document the artist's dilemmas of choice and decision."[2]

Still maintaining the spontaneity and large scale of the Abstract Expressionists, a group of artists began to deal more extensively with vast areas or fields of color. Rather than the suggestion of shallow or ephemeral space, this

Color-field movement stressed the two-dimensional element inherent in painting.

Therefore, although influenced by Pollock's exploitation of the accident and overall size, Helen Frankenthaler began to stain her canvases with diluted paint creating large and fluid color areas suggestive of landscapes. Like Pollock, she works with her canvas on the floor, pouring on the paint and spontaneously spreading around the medium. Since the paint is thinned, it is literally soaked up by the unprimed canvas. Not only is there a fusion of paint and canvas with no separation of image from ground, but also the flow of the wash-like paint creates rich areas of luminous and lucious form and colors.

Utilizing acrylic wash and the soak-stain process, a deliberate and distinct separation between color, line and ground occurs in the work of Suzanne Jackson. By control and restriction of the stain within delineated boundaries, she confines her images to certain sections of the surface rather than an overall working of space. Her use of unprimed canvas is approached traditionally as it acts as the surface on which the image is placed, not as a component which acts with color in order to define the form and character of her imagery. Color ceases to define form but acts as an element which enhances the character and emotive qualities of her imagery when contained within the structural boundaries. Her imagery is personal to the extent of being esoteric. Distorted yet recognizable figural forms interact within vignettes presenting the viewer with seemingly symbolic and spiritual narratives.

The heart shape and the bird are recurrent images in her work. Often their shape will be distorted suggesting other objects and images. In addition, they define the boundaries of the figure which become clarified through internal line and color variations.

In *Witches, Bitches, and Loons, 1972* (fig. 2), a transparent figure of acrylic wash acts as the ground in which the two central figures interact. These figures take structural form inside the transparent figure and are outlined by a heart-shape which finds its point by the extending hand of the transparent ground. These heads become more literal through line drawings of facial features. The bird is repeated on both sides of the central figures. Maintaining its basic shape and interior, the wings are extended into flower-like appendages on one side. On the other, the flower-like wings are more prominant as the body of the bird is distorted and subdued by an almost complete dilution of the pigment wash.

Jackson's work until 1975 left large unpainted areas of canvas creating an almost isolated relationship between the image and its surface. Since that time Jackson's work has been executed in an overall spatial and expressionistic manner reminiscent of earlier Color-field painters. While color areas are more prominant and visually freer, they still do not define form but rather act as an atmospheric component in the gestural and expansive use of pigment and canvas.

In *Splash, 1976* (pl. 2), Jackson retains the heart-shape making it the central area of ground. Color and unprimed canvas interact to define the internal and external boundaries of the shape. A second red heart, while distorted, acts as a repetitive element which recurs in Jackson's earlier works. The fish, although linearly defined, is transversed by gestural and "splashy" color which intersects and flows into the overall outside areas of the heart-shape.

Morris Louis also incorporated a staining technique in his work. "The thinned oil-compatible acrylic paint . . . was poured onto unprimed cotton duck canvas . . . that had been draped and partly stapled to a rectangular frame or scaffolding either propped against the wall or up off the floor. Both the frame and the loose canvas itself could be moved to control the flow of pigment as it streamed down the canvas, and Louis sometimes used a stick wrapped in gauze to further direct the flow . . ."[3] This procedure allowed Louis full control of his paint throughout the process.

Louis painted in series, exploring, modifying and perfecting his art. In his Unfurls Series, 1960-1961, different colors, sometimes contrasting, were poured from the edges diagonally toward the bottom of the canvas as if being drawn by gravity. The center is devoid of color. Even though empty, the center is as important a component of the works and as evocative as the multi-colored stripes.

Frank Bowling began to use the staining technique extensively upon his arrival in New York from London in 1966. Although the tormented expressionist image, dominant in his previous work, was not banished completely, a new freedom and feel for lustrous color enhanced Bowling's paintings.

From 1966 to 1971 the map, usually of South America or of his native country, Guyana, became a recurrent theme in Bowling's work, and he utilized both the staining technique and silk screening. The lustrous flow of colors gradually began to rule the canvas and take precedence over the image, eventually eliminating it altogether.

In the early 1970s, Bowling started pouring his paint directly onto the canvas as it lay on the floor or on a low platform. With this new freedom, the stream of colors began to take on a will of its own and Bowling began taking his cues from the flow of paint rather than dictating its course. The paintings from this period exude a new looseness in technique with the ebullient profusion of highly keyed colors radiating from the canvas. The medium in some areas seems to be more diluted than it previously had been so the paint seems to soak into the canvas to a greater extentcreating a lyrical wash effect. This dreamy sensuality is heightened by the strong sense of color with an increased sophisticated feel for the surface qualities.

In the last two years, Bowling has begun to work on a new series of paintings in which a geyser-like rush of colors gushes upward amidst a thinly washed background (fig. 3). There is an unsettling thrust to Bowling's work as the interior amalgam of poured colors seemingly splits open and disrupts the soft, serene background field.

Bowling is above all a colorist. Throughout his career from his expressionistic figural work done in London in the 1960s to his current statements, color has been an overriding concern. "Color for me is very personal . . . Color is a sense of a very personal dilemma. I'm adjusting color almost entirely through emotional leads. Color plays an enormous part in my work, if not the most important."[4] (pl. 3)

Inspired by the natural phenomena around her in her Washington neighborhood and in the more rural environ-

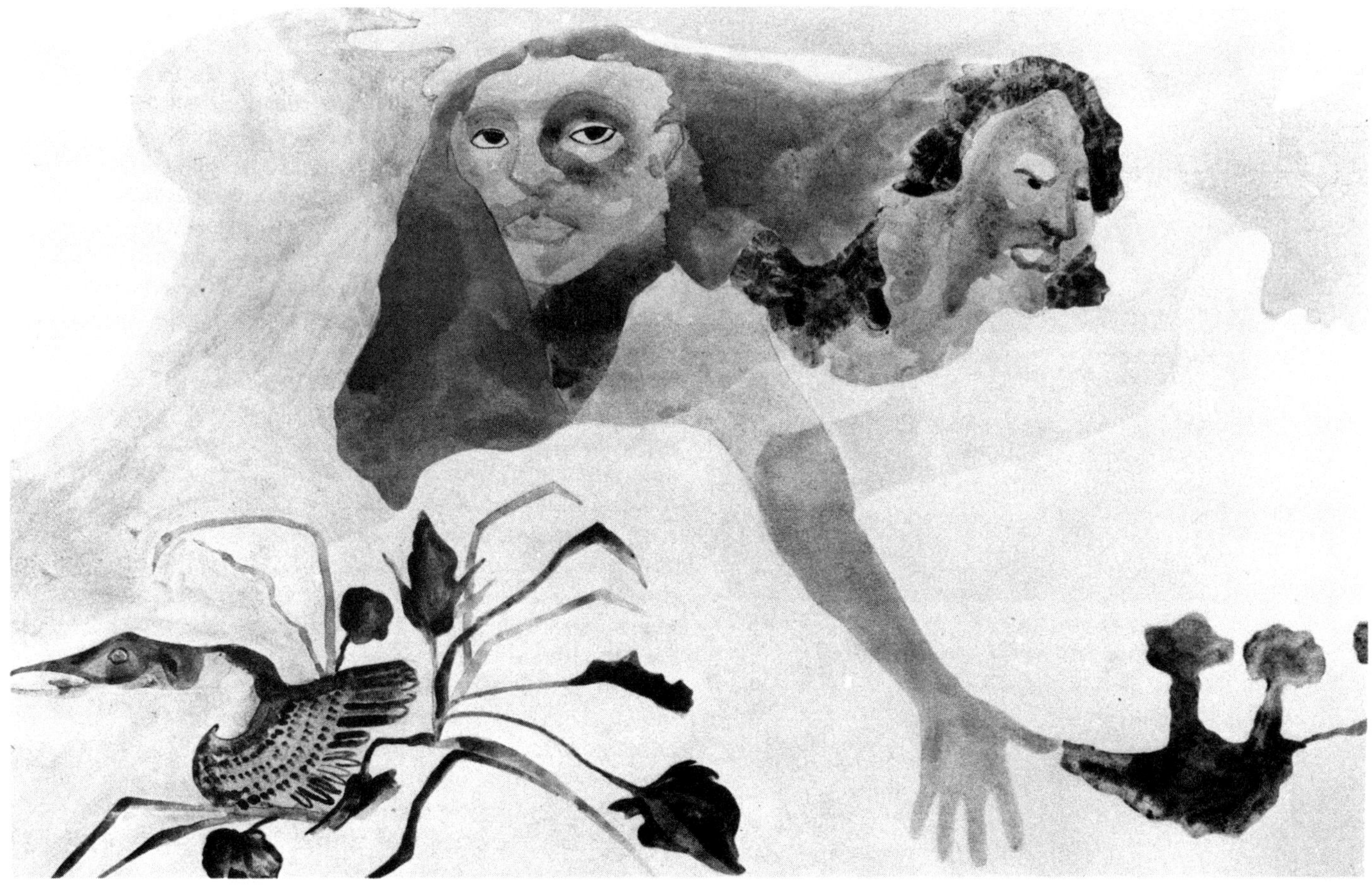

2. SUZANNE JACKSON. *Witches, Bitches and Loons. 1972*

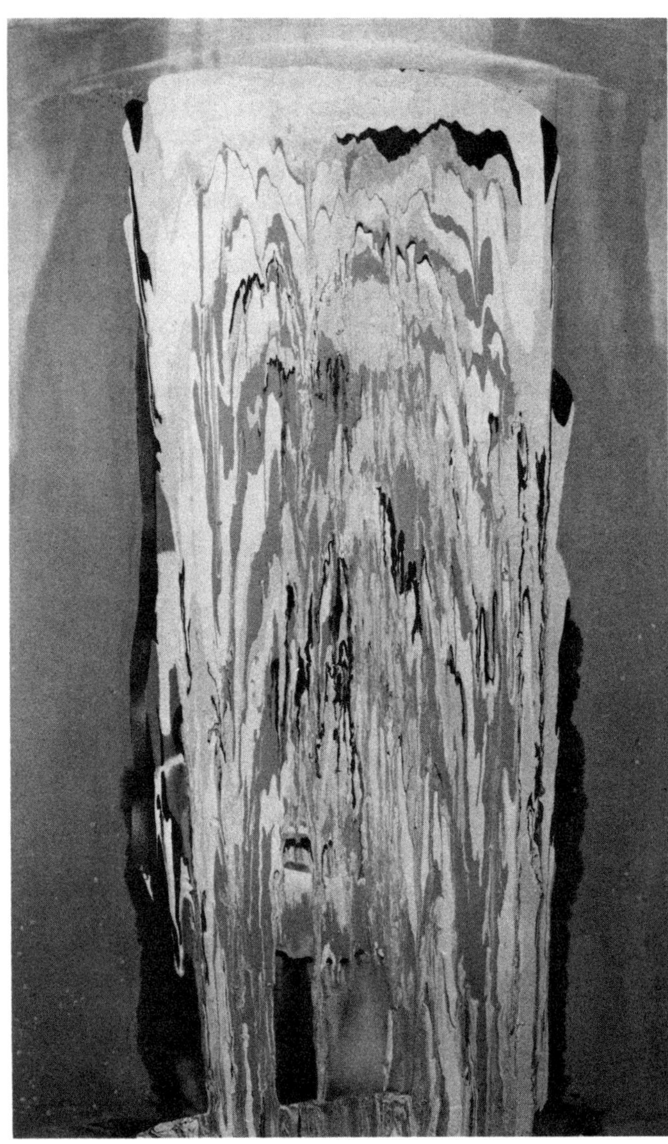

3. FRANK BOWLING. *Cathedral. 1975*

ment of her childhood, Alma Thomas transforms these tangible realities into dabs of small colored tesserae, suggesting a mosaic-like effect. The origin of the subject is merely hinted at by the rhythmic floating forms, sensitive colors and explicit titles.

There is an underlying organized structure within the work that acts as a counterpoint and restraint to the prevailing essence of lightheartedness. Within this framework, colors react and respond to each other and their placement on the canvas, and the patches themselves seem to whirl in place without shattering the tight organized network.

Upon his arrival in Washington in 1962, Sam Gilliam's work began to move away from a figural art to a more powerful abstraction that exploited the inherent and unique qualities of paint on canvas.

Gilliam's paintings in the mid 1960s were stained to a rich, luminous glow. The paint soaked into the canvas and the medium was no longer a skin to be peeled away, but became one with its backing. Furthermore, the canvas was not used as a mere receptacle for the paint, but became an active participant in the process. The artist folded and crumpled the canvas while the paint was not yet dry, creating compelling and surprising blends and bleedings of the applied color (fig. 4).

As a natural progression to this handling of the canvas, and as a response to his surroundings, Gilliam freed the canvas from the stretcher. "What was most personal to me were the things I saw in my own environment—such as clotheslines filled with clothes with so much weight that they had to propped up."[5] Gilliam began to treat the canvas as fabric to be draped, suspended or laid on the floor and, as a result, his work no longer functioned two-dimensionally but now could explore the environmental space around it, giving the luminous color a greater chance to explode and erupt. The nuances that occur from these expanded possibilities are many, and they function to enhance the rich color relationships and formal factors abundant in Gilliam's paintings.

In the mid 1970s, Gilliam enlarged on the notion of the independence of the canvas, and the use of the canvas as an integral and active element in the art itself. By suspending the work from hangers and adding zippers, buttons and other clothing accessories to it, he increased the role of the canvas as material in an almost Dadaist juxtaposition.

Reacting against and perhaps challenging the prevalency

of the gestural in the art of the late 1940s and early 1950s, Barnett Newman's edges are clearly and sharply defined and the paint is applied in a smooth, even manner. Newman "articulate(d) the surface of the painting as a 'field,' rather than as a composition . . . He wanted the rectangle of the canvas to determine the pictorial structure."[6] Stripes, or "zips" as Newman called them, move either horizontally or vertically across the canvas dividing the color field. These zips vary in hue and width. Subtle changes take place in the relationship between field and neighboring zip as these variances occur. Space is ambiguous and the viewer can read the zips as the focal points of the canvas with the color field as background or the field as the chief component with the zips merely used as accents.

Ad Reinhardt reduced his canvas to a nearly minimal austerity. His doctrine was less is more and he followed twelve rules: no texture; no brushwork; no sketching; no forms; no design; no colors ("Color blinds."); no light; no space; no time; no size or scale; no movement; and no object, no subject, no matter."[7]

Reinhardt is, perhaps, best known for his black canvases of the 1950s in which he juxtaposed various shades of black tones. One has to look at these paintings at close range in order to distinguish shapes and tonal variations. His canvases are reduced to the most simple and severe forms and colors.

James Little combines the more controlled brushwork and even application of paint on canvas, evident in the works of Newman and Reinhardt, with the freedom of gestural abandon. Little, however, stresses the physicality of the painting process, as did the Abstract Expressionists, examining and exploring the many possibilities and the varied qualities of his materials. Little explains that "painting ought to be about the paint . . . what you can do with materials."[8] His paintings reflect this concern with paint and the application of the medium to the surface, and because of these sensibilities Little refers to himself as a surface painter.

Little works with the format of a gestural and painterly color field bordered by two symmetrical stripes, either along the horizontal or vertical framing edge. These stripes are not only a different color from the field, but are also painted precisely and meticulously. The juxtaposition of colors becomes jolting at times, as well as the contrast of painting styles within one canvas. Whereas the Abstract Expressionists' gestures and brush strokes seem to extend beyond the boundaries of their works, Little encloses, almost imprisons, his active, brushy surface with the bordering stripes.

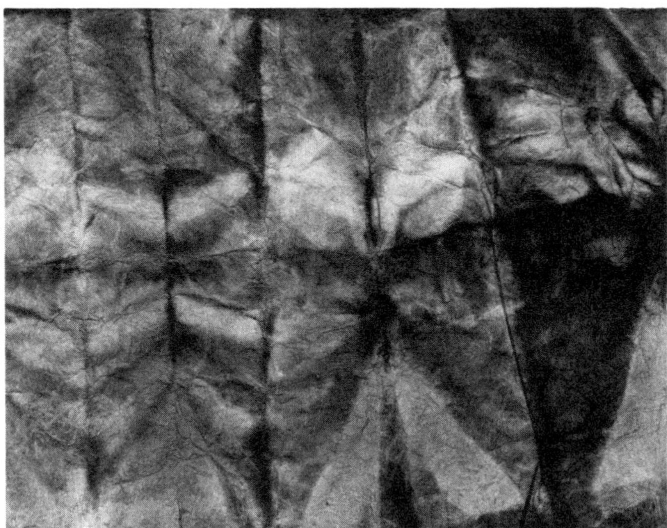

4. SAM GILLIAM. *Untitled. 1971*

These techniques and color relationships are well thought out in advance, although Little allows for a certain amount of invention as the work proceeds. All of his surfaces are executed differently since Little is interested in the painterliness of each particular paint mixture. The artist explains that the large field of color can sometimes reflect his mood and then he will decide the color for the stripes by testing, scraping out and occasionally discarding it altogether.

The juxtaposition of the organic with the geometric creates a dichotomy between objectivity and emotion. Little's paintings are, therefore, difficult to decipher, but convey a deep sensibility toward surface, texture and color.

Little's drawings, however, break out of the constraints of the bordering stripes without losing the composition's sense of order and balance (fig. 5 and 6). By nature of the ink medium and its adaptability to gradual and subtle tonal variations, Little sponges off excess ink achieving sensitive and lyric blendings from dark to light.

Although sharing a certain commonality with the ab-

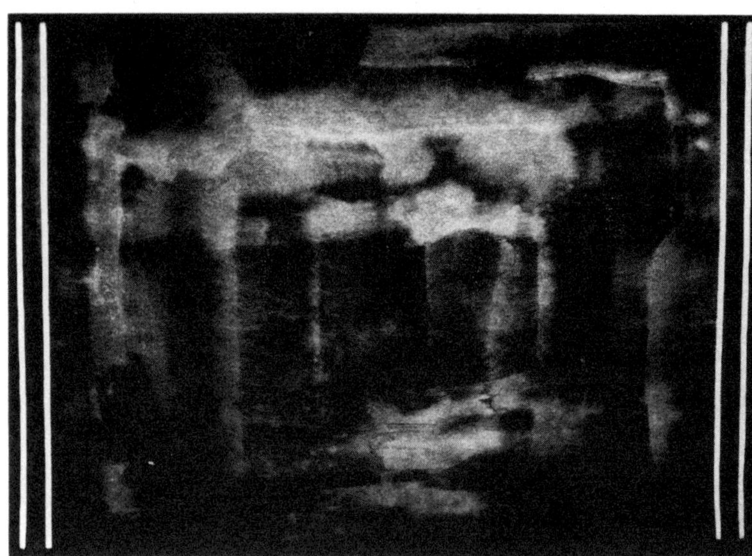

5. JAMES LITTLE. *Dark Cloud Passing Before the Sun. 1977*

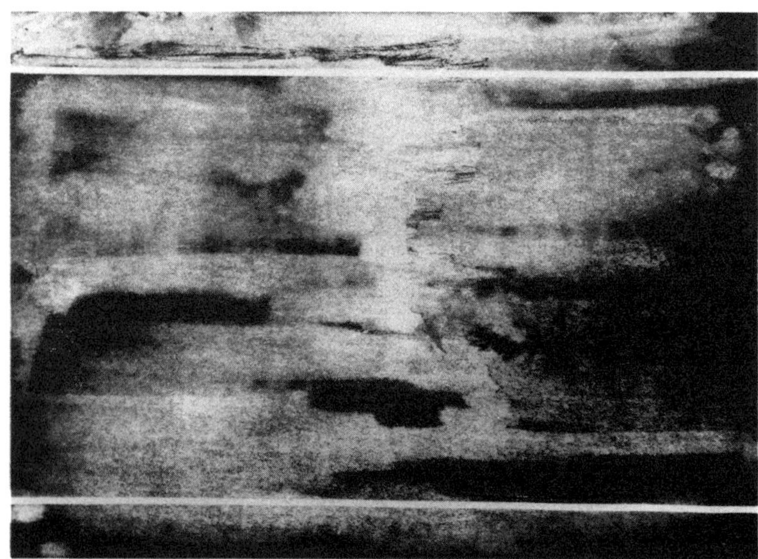

6. JAMES LITTLE. *Overtures. 1977*

stract expressionist and color-field movements, a system of painting, Hard-edge art, arose that challenged many aspects of those two earlier styles. The expressive and personal use of paint on canvas, and the spontaneous, accidental quality of the work gave way to a flat and even application of the paint medium. Furthermore, boundaries between each color and shape were distinct and clear, unlike the ambiguous spatial renderings found in those previous movements. Because of these clean edges, the works took on a geometric theme. Scale, however, remained large but no longer did the viewer feel surrounded or enveloped by the work since the intimate quality is abandoned in favor of a more objective, straightforward approach.

Having worked with Morris Louis in developing new approaches to stain procedures, Kenneth Noland began to utilize the center of the canvas as a structuring device in the early 1960s. The artist depicted forms related to the shape of the canvas through a shared central axis. This schematic arrangement excluded the possibility of arbitrary decisions and freed Noland's use of color. In 1963-1964 he developed the chevron motif and by 1967 had reduced the format of his painting to horizontal color stripes often on extremely long canvases.

Al Loving moved to New York in the late 1960s from his native Detroit to set up a personal communication with and exposure to Frank Stella and Kenneth Noland, Hard-edge artists with whom he felt a kinship. Loving acquired a loft studio which he felt changed his concept of space, and his work accordingly increased in scale.

Loving began to paint nine foot cubes which progressed to geometrically shaped works made up of separate canvases strung together. A thirty-five foot work made up of ninety-one individual canvases was exhibited at the Whitney Museum in New York City in 1969. After his exhibition, Loving decided to deal with the immediacy of color application rather than with its manipulation for illusionistic effects.

He worked in the more constricted confines of the Hard-edge idiom for a short time before rediscovering his interest in serendipity. Naming Abstract Expressionism as the primary influence in his work, Loving stresses the importance of spontaneity in process and visual perception when he said, "I'm thinking all the time, always changing. I try to control the events or define them, but the process finds the truth."[9]

In 1972, Loving began exploring new possibilities that

were in direct opposition to his hard-edged work, returning to a looser abstraction. He began to paint, dye and dunk strips of material, then sewed them together and hung them from the ceiling, nailed them to the walls, laid them on the floor, or draped them over pipes. This new-found freedom and expressionistic reversal was also translated to cardboard and paper (fig. 7). Expanding the freedom of his expression, he began exploring and manipulating space, in all its aspects, as well as the ongoing composing of the work rather than the ultimate work itself.

Loving has since come full circle and returned to the stretched canvas with a new interest in illusionism and spatial consideration. As a result of his experience with strips of cardboard, Loving now incorporates torn paper in the canvas surface adding another dimension to the pictorial space. This method is employed in his recent Water Lily Series (pl. 4). The paper, acting as the lilies, creates a feeling of suspension across the canvas.

In the early 1960s, Frank Stella pioneered the concept of the shaped canvas as an echo of the geometry of its interior design. To eliminate "leftover space" in his Aluminum Series, he cut out notches from the canvas. This was followed with more extreme shaping in the Copper Series. Stella began to paint multi-colored canvases which culminated in the late 1960s in the curvilinear designs of the Protractor Series. This consisted of thirty-one different themes, each with three variations—interlacings, rainbows and fans. Stella used commercial fluorescent polymer paint which gives his canvases a rich, luminous quality. The effect of color and design makes a strong and immediate impression on the viewer's eye. The paint is applied with large brushes in a flat manner leaving no trace of a personal handwriting.

Moving toward a more refined geometric, hard-edged style in the mid 1960s was William T. Williams who had previously been involved in an expressionistic technique while a graduate student at Yale University. He was concerned with proportion and balance and influenced by the Constructivists such as Malevich. A high keyed sense of color played an important role in this development, so that by 1968 Williams had expanded his palette to include a metallic paint.

Elbert Jackson L.A.M.F. Part II (fig. 8) exemplifies the components of Williams' art at this time. Geometric configurations prevail, but the intricate overlapping and strong diagonals, as well as the dissonant color add dynamism and rhythmic fluidity that supercede the more dispassionate, meticulous application of paint on the canvas. The surface is highly active and expressionistic without the expressionists' gestural brush work (pl. 5).

In the late 1960s, Williams became interested in public art and through the Smokehouse Group he was able to design murals for the outer walls of buildings in New York City. This experience afforded Williams a larger and more massive surface on which to work.

In the early 1970s, Williams started a series of paintings quite different from those executed in previous years. The hard-edged geometry was forsaken for a delicate repetitive pattern that ran horizontally across the canvas. A pleasing illusionistic decorative quality is achieved, but Williams soon returned to a geometric abstraction illuminating the textural qualities of the surface and dealing with closer tonal values between colors. Williams again uses large geometric areas defined by color. Each of these areas, however, is faceted, and juxtaposes a vivid color with a more muted shade creating a rippling, active surface. Many of these paintings are done in a monochromatic scheme resulting in a more subtle utilization of tonal and surface variations.

At present Williams has returned to the horizontal-vertical axis after twelve years of employing the diagonal. In addition, a painterliness and illusionism has been reintroduced to the new work which promises to be an integral and important phase in Williams' career. Although these recent paintings are seemingly more expressionistic, Williams tries not to work out of pure emotion since he does not want to act as a protagonist for his work, hoping each piece will communicate its own universal truth.

His primary objective has been to make the work look on canvas the way it looks in his head, discounting for himself the Abstract Expressionists' exploitation of the momentary action. "As you get older there's no such thing as spontaneity . . . I create the accident."[10]

An interest in optical sensation was explored in a 1965 exhibition, "The Responsive Eye," at The Museum of Modern Art in New York City. Some of the artists represented in the show are classified as Optical or Op artists. They "depend on close value color contrasts, after-images, and subliminal color effects, all of which are designed to stress the importance of the art of perception itself."[11]

It is difficult to focus on a single point in many of these optical paintings; the seeming pulsations and movements on the still canvas strain the eyes, creating sometimes unpleasant and eerie sensations. Furthermore, although many similarities can be drawn between Hard-edge and Op art (such as application of paint or clearly defined color areas), by the use of flickering, illusionistic devices, the practitioner of Op art destroys the flatness of the two-dimensional canvas, a concept all important to the Hard-edge artist.

Between 1962 and 1967, Larry Poons explored the optical sensations aroused by painting many small, elliptical dots in a grid-like network against a field of contrasting colors. The ovoid dots then play on the viewer's eye creating an after-image. One sees dots where they do not actually exist, against the background field or even on the adjoining wall as they seemingly dance upon the canvas.

An optical art vocabulary is found in Sharon Sutton's early work executed in the first part of the 1970s. Contrasts of black and white and spatial illusionism, reminiscent of the paintings of England's Bridget Riley, are stressed, rather than a penchant for eye fatigue and after-images. In the ensuing years, Sutton's colors have taken on a more muted tonal quality of earthy blends and progressions. The undulating surface gives way to a smooth, rhythmic flow of one compositional element to another as in *This Box Is Our Box, 1972* (fig. 9).

This lithograph may be viewed as a whole with a pinwheel shape against a background, or the work can be broken down to squares, parallelograms, and triangular shapes. This can further be broken down to the elemental rectilinear grid surrounding the circles. In addition, rectangles become parallelograms and circles become ellipses suggesting an illusionistic perspective.

The use of repetitive geometric elements and the prevailing mode of expression in Sutton's works constitute the universal truth of the order and discipline that has to be contended with and confronted in one's everyday existence. An architectonic format and a rectangular grid reappear frequently in Sutton's prints. The impact of the exacting repetitive organization of her work is a result of an enormous capability for self-control and patience which she attributes to the discipline of her architectural background.

Fading of That Fabulous Olden Lady (pl. 6) uses this grid motif, albeit slightly warped and distorted. The circles within the grid network remain straightforward and erect almost as if encouraging the weakening structure to withstand the invisible forces descending upon it. As strength gives way to vulnerability, the viewer is able to admire the courage and forbearance of the "fabulous olden lady" of the title.

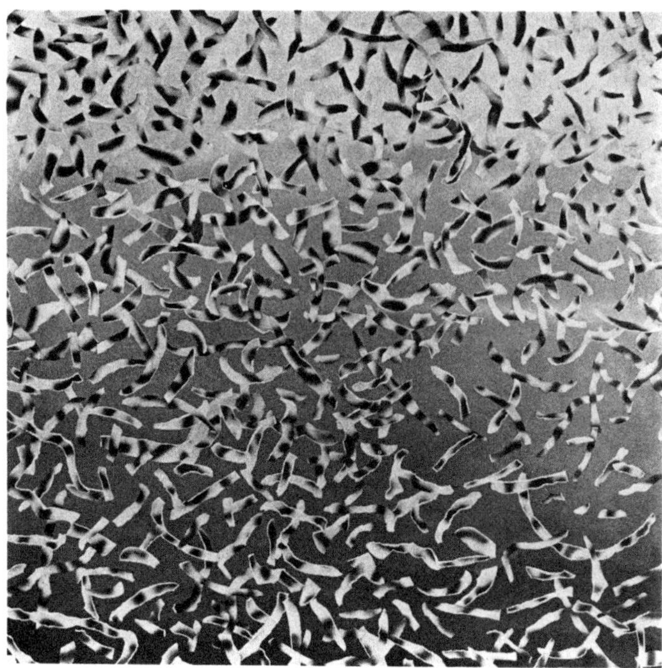

7. AL LOVING. *Untitled.*

Sutton stresses the importance of the title, usually poetic, to the viewer as a literal link to the art object's visual content. She readily admits this need to communicate to her audience. This exchange and viewer enlightenment become the artist's primary interest, in both her fine art work and her architectural projects. "I am interested in getting others interested in their own creative problem solving process, rather than in making an art which communicate(s) my process."[12] Sutton brings her skills and her personality to the work and feels that the audience brings in its own experiential base creating a necessary communicative interplay between the two.

Recently, Sutton has incorporated the use of material in her prints. The pattern of the fabric is carefully selected to emphasize further the pictorial image as well as add new dimension to the visual plane. The overall structure is geometric and formal, but the subtlety of the line and fabric add to the choreography of the rhythm and sensuality.

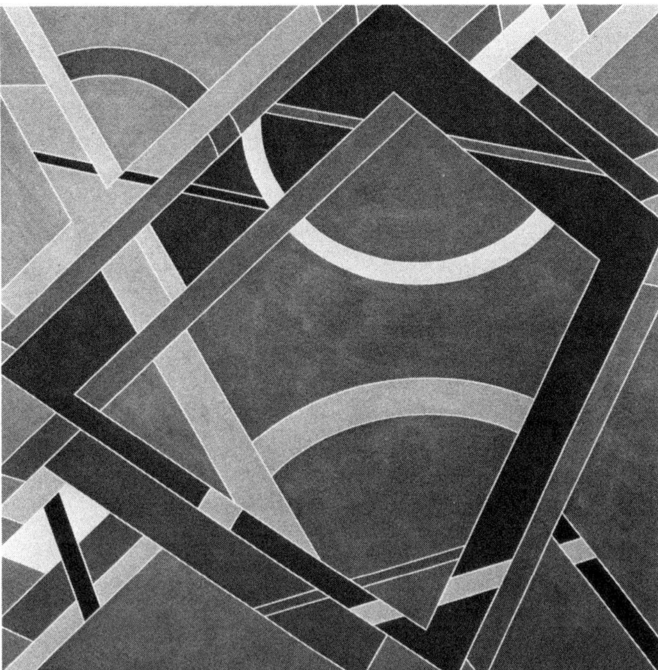

8. WILLIAM T. WILLIAMS. *Elbert Jackson, L.A.M.F. Part II. 1969*

9. SHARON SUTTON. *This Box Is Our Box. 1972*

Fred Eversley's sculpture explores the questions of optics and perception three-dimensionally. He retains the concept of kinetic art without using mechanical movement or artificial light changes. Employing a scientific method of polyester compound casting which involves the spinning of the material until it hardens, Eversley achieves these objectives. Thus, the surface and media itself radiate a kinetic effect when exposed to natural changes in light, the environment and the spectator.

Eversley's first series of sculptures, executed from 1968 to 1971 were cast in a cylindrical mold in three layers, using the same three transparent colors in an identical sequence. Although given these constants, by manipulating and altering the amount of each color poured, and by the ultimate cutting of the basic cylindrical mold to various shapes, Eversley was able to create highly individualistic pieces.

Eversley has concentrated in the ensuing years on both simpler forms, primarily parabolic and circular discs, and on a reduction of color, concentrating on black, white and gray. This work is exemplified in *Untitled #9* (fig. 10). Seen merely as a work of art it is a haunting, singular statement of pristine simplicity. However, upon closer inspection its highly polished surface mirrors not only its environment, but also mirrors the spectator although, because of its concavity, in an inverted, slightly distorted way. As one moves, the reflections on the sculpture change. The work therefore establishes a unique relationship with the viewer, as each person brings to the work his/her own unique set of experiences.

So Eversley's sculptures work on two levels, scientifically and aesthetically, as a sophisticated engineered product exploiting the environmental and perceptual responses of the viewer, and also as a highly polished, exquisite piece of art, admired for its gracefulness and purity. This duality of purpose is confirmed by the artist who wrote, "Art to me should ideally be universal in content, understanding, and appeal . . . . and actively interact with and involve the spectator and his environment . . . I am dealing with real energies, forces, space, time and matter."[13]

While not optical, Melvin Edwards' sculptures are concerned with the viewers' involvement and interaction with their environment. These works favor a linear continuity that encourages spatial flow in many directions while at the same time acknowledging the securing force of gravity (fig. 11). Edwards works with a variety of materials from heavy, yet seductive, welded steel to the diaphanous, yet

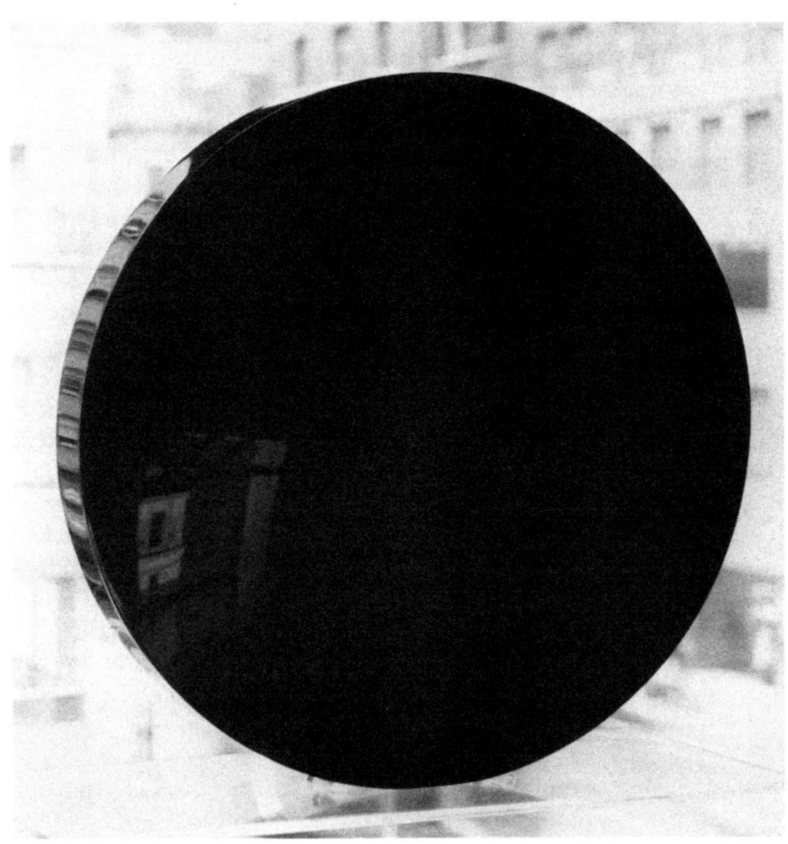

10. FRED EVERSLEY. *Untitled #9. 1975*

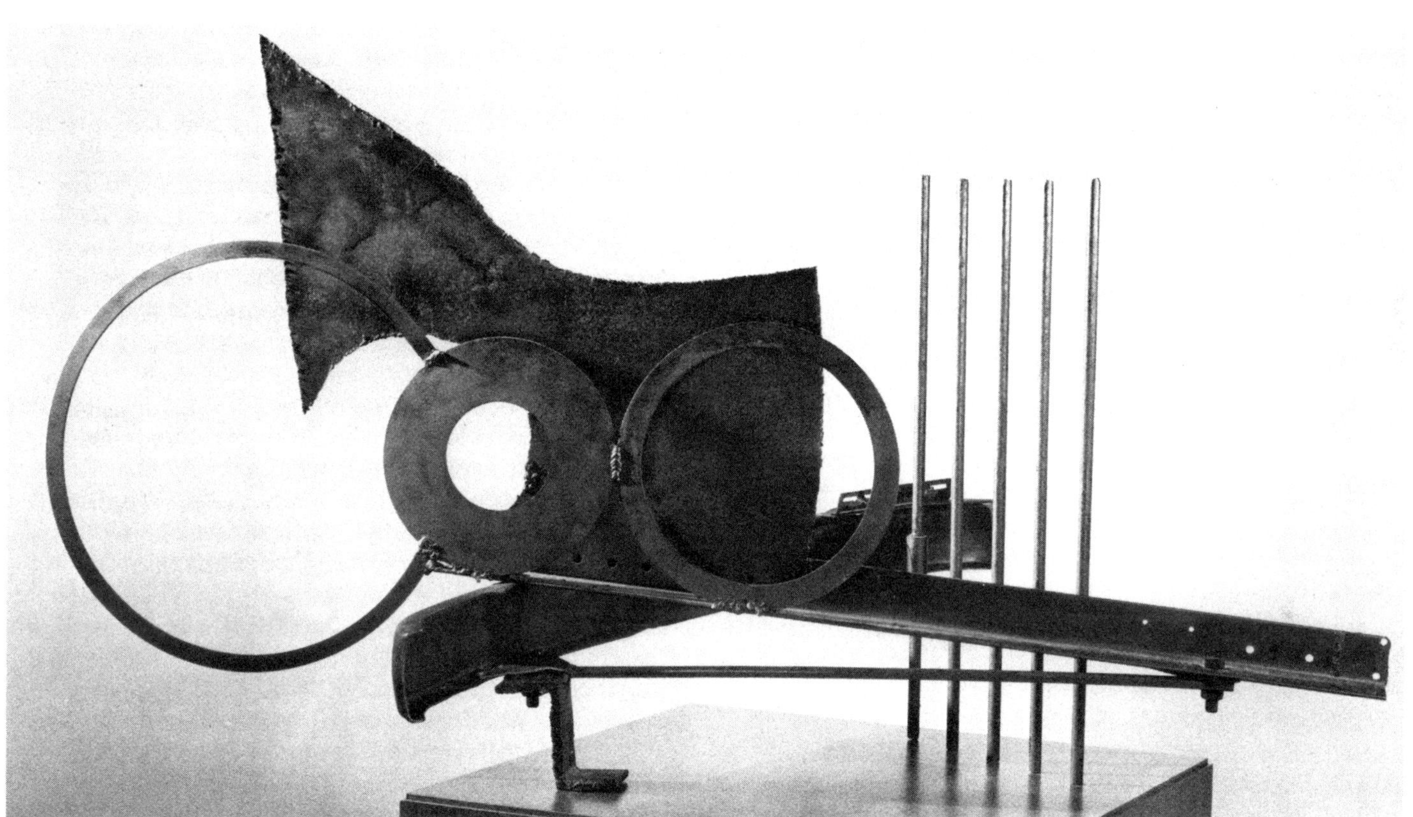

11. MEL EDWARDS. *The Fourth Circle. 1966*

inherently dangerous, barbed wire. The three-dimensional structures reach out and define the space they inhabit. In addition to his interest in the object itself and its surroundings, the surface qualities, painted or polished, of the work receive the artist's consideration and attention.

These interests, particularly the development of space, has led Edwards to explore several motifs, such as the circle. *Double Circle,* an eight foot sculpture, was installed at Lenox Avenue and 144th Street in 1970. The sculpture consists of four circles, yellow on one side, silver on the other. An interplay of color and surface is created as the painted yellow plane is reflected on the silver surface. The reverse is true as well. By changing one's position, the viewer's perception of the object and the urban environment is changed.

In the Rocker Series, a salute to his grandmother, Edwards sliced the circle in half. The semi-circle lies with the arc side down. An eight-by-ten foot rocker piece appeared in the 1970 Whitney Museum Sculpture Annual. To create a variety of effects, chains of both galvanized and unplated steel run across the open arms of the sculpture. Furthermore, each plane of the rocker was painted in varying shades of red which were applied in different modes from smooth non-brush effects to a gestural and expressionistic paint handling.

The triangle, another motif utilized by Edwards, is found in *Try-Try* (pl. 7). The sculpture consists of four triangles with short elements extending from the top point. Edwards employs chains on these appendages, not only as an aesthetic device but also to structurally create an opposite pull, thus keeping the triangles upright.

From 1969 onward, Edwards began to work extensively with barbed wire. He was attracted primarily to its linearity and environmental possibilities. Although the wire is commonplace material, it offers an ambiguous and even provocative quality leading Edwards to exploit its lyrical potential as a line in space, creating three-dimensional drawings.

Edwards created a forty foot long curtain of barbed wire for the 5 + 1 exhibition at the State University of New York at Stony Brook in 1969. The curtain was suspended from the ceiling and came to about four inches from the floor. Although the viewer could see the works on the other side of the room, the curtain was impenetrable and entry could be gained only by leaving the gallery and passing through another door. The barbed wire confronted and challenged the viewer, and isolated and imprisoned the space.

Edwards has stated that he lives his life around the idea of making sculpture,[14] and this dynamism of purpose is matched by the dynamic execution and spatial considerations in his work. Conscious of the viewers' response and their feelings toward their environmental space, Edwards strives toward making sculpture on a scale that would emphasize the three-dimensionality of the aesthetic experience. Thus, the sculpture would become more architectural in size as well as in impact.

During the late 1950s, an art form emerged which focused on the interrelationship between art and life through the compositional integration of materials and objects which were iconographic of urban life and mass culture. Termed Junk Art or Neo-Dada, the movement's predetermined selection of literal images (symbols, readymades and debris) is depersonalized and objectively portrayed and provide a contrast to the personal, spontaneous and expressive recordings of the Abstract Expressionists.

These easily recognizable everyday objects provided a reference point enabling immediate associations. The objects exist virtually without transformation, presenting factual information concerning their particular life cycles. Materials, structure, texture and color are predominant in the artists' intent. Unlike the Pop artists who followed, the Neo-Dadaists, particularly Jasper Johns and Robert Rauschenberg, emphasize the illumination of the painting process, often achieved through visual effects reminiscent of the Abstract Expressionists.

While certain associations exist between the type of objects employed by the Neo-Dadaists and the preceeding Dadaists, distinctions are apparent. Generally, the Dadaists were proponents of art as life. Thus the object, in an untransformed state, was elevated to a state of art by the "choice" of the artist. Choice became the process. The Neo-Dadaists were more concerned with the differences between life and art. Through the interweaving and incorporation of the art process with the untransformed object, the artist exists as a bond between the two. Or as stated by Rauschenberg, "Painting relates to both art and life. Neither can be made. (I try to act in the gap between the two.)"[15]

The selection of symbols and objects primarily for their structural and textural qualities results in a detached and impersonal usage in these compositions. While by definition, these objects provide referential connotations, the nature of their use by these artists is void of any intended commentary or subjective statement.

Pop art as a viable movement emerged in New York City during the early 1960s with such practitioners as Roy Lichtenstein, Andy Warhol and Claes Oldenburg. The Pop artist concerned himself not with obtuse elitist statements, but rather with identifiable images. Roy Lichtenstein stated that "Pop art looks out into the world; it appears to accept its environment, which is not good or bad, but different, another state of mind."[16] It is with this commitment to the implications of the popular mass-produced culture that the Pop Art movement took root.

Roy Lichtenstein is known primarily for his works based on the comic strip. He does not simply enlarge the image, but actively and purposefully selects and abstracts the qualities he wants for his own work. "Unification is in fact the key to his work. He omits distracting details, lines, figures, or words that destroy form in his sources and presents that form, rearranged in its ultimate clarity . . . Lichtenstein generalizes, reduces, and simplifies."[17] The importance of the comic strip is that the characters are everyman in his most simplistic form. Also, the large scale generalizes this commonness all the more.

In "The Store," an exhibition by Claes Oldenburg in the early 1960s, soft sculptures of common food items such as a hamburger and a piece of cake were displayed. Oldenburg enlarged the scale of these everyday objects to giant proportions reflecting the obsessions that Americans have with big and powerful things, whether they be buildings, countries or sculptures. These sculptures were made of hand-sewn canvas and are loosely stuffed. The softness of the sculpture makes the object able to be pinched, poked and flattened, something impossible with a metal or wood sculpture. These qualities of familiarity and malleability allow the spectator to view the sculpture in a more direct fashion without the usual fence of detachment that so often exists between audience and object.

Remnants of the Abstract Expressionist influence can be found in Oldenburg's soft sculptures. He drips and splashes paint on the canvas skin of these works. This technique emphasizes the surface quality of the work, as well as its informality.

Andy Warhol isolates his image whether it be Brillo boxes or a portrait of Marilyn Monroe. His subjects are presented impersonally and without comment, either positive or negative. Warhol does not intrude upon the viewer nor does he intend to preach about modern life. At times, his images, some of unpleasant subjects such as Jackie Kennedy on the day of the President's assassination, are repeated on a single canvas, dulling the inherent repugnant flavor of the work. Warhol claims "when you see a gruesome picture over and over again, it doesn't really have any effect."[18]

Although incorporating the commercially recognized objects found in Pop, a group of artists began to infuse their work with a renewed interest in and feel for painterly techniques. No longer were the images icons of contemporary society; instead they had become a part of the expressionistic gestural totality of the work. Rather than being an offshoot of Pop Art, this style had its roots in Dada and Surrealism, and more recently in Neo-Dada.

Jim Dine has focused many of his series on one particular object, exploring it in various media and forms. The object is not portrayed in a cool, impersonal manner, but because of the energetic and unabandoned use of materials, the works exude a passion not found in Pop.

Larry Rivers also uses recognizable images in his works. However, he looks not to contemporary society for them, but goes back to historical references, most particularly in the series, Dutch Masters, 1963 and Rainbow Rider, 1977, both derived from Rembrandt. Rivers' brush strokes rush freely across the canvas through the images, sometimes distorting, disguising or even obliterating them.

Thus the artist and viewer are apt to get as involved with the technique just as well as with the subject matter. Space is left for personal observations and interpretations. This is also apparent in the works of Raymond Saunders.

Over the last ten years, Saunders has dealt increasingly in his works with an abundance of images, both pictorial and written, in a free associative manner. Furthermore, his paintings take on many drawing characteristics because of Saunders' use of incised lines. Conversely, his many drawings have a loose flowing feel reminiscent of paint handling.

The image of Mickey Mouse appears, at first, to dominate *Dr. Jesus* (fig. 12), but there are so many other elements at play that one's interest is immediately diverted to all areas of the canvas. The bold, brushy application of paint is in direct contrast to the traditional cartoon book rendering of Mickey. A bright red dominates the work with strong accents of blue and black. Stenciled letters and numbers, usually in sequence, are seen throughout floating in and out of the heavily painted surface. God is spelled out a number of times, and appears at one point directly over Mickey's head. This, perhaps, comments on the association of the popular cartoon character with the word, God, and with the Dr. Jesus of the title. A halo of stars emphasizes the point. The word, God, is transposed to the word, good. In direct contrast to this sentiment, however, is the phrase "Rat on Mickey" barely visible at the right of the mouse's leg.

Themes and images, such as numbers and letters, hearts and Walt Disney characters, recur throughout Saunders' work. The cross also reappears frequently as in *1,2,3,4,5* (fig. 13). Not portrayed in a formal sense, the large cross appears more as the intersecting of two brush strokes than as a religious symbol. A series of dotted lines spewing forth from the top of the vertical axis of the cross and the incomplete phrase "first church of" add to the irreligious and playful nature of the work.

Space is undefined. Collage elements and incised, draughtsman-like lines are scattered across the canvas in what appears to be a spontaneous manner. The seeming random placement of lines and splotchy appearance of some areas of paint affect a childlike naivete.

The iconography and references in many of Saunders' works seem deliberately esoteric and personal. This allows room, however, for the viewer to bring to the work his/her own interpretation and connotation.

In a response to the personal, esoteric and referential nature of art and the primary focus of artists for interpretation, expression and definition, a style developed in the mid 1960s which espoused the ultimate condition of art to exist in and of itself without external determinants or emotional influence or stimuli. Termed Minimal, it focuses primarily on description, rather than interpretation, of the states and conditions in which the art object exists. These descriptions are literal, eliminating the narrative, and exposing the phenomenal and perceptual factors and elements of the visual experience. Many of the Minimalists were critics and writers[19] and adhered to the existential belief that existence precedes essence, yet they differ from existentialists since they do not believe that definitions are possible, just facts and conditions of existence.[20]

Minimalists work primarily in three dimensions allowing "real" rather than illusionary space and conditions. By eliminating parts to emphasize the whole[21] they develop gestalts which will provide total visual information. The use of elementary geometric forms allows the image to be coextensive with its structure. In many cases the artist designs plans which are industrially executed in order to eliminate any traces of the artists' "handwriting." To accentuate further the autonomous and isolated conditions in which the object exists, the Minimalists do not title the works to avoid any possible external connection or reference. Their concern is to provide immediate correlations and distinctions between the ideal concept of the form and the real "existence" of form in three dimension.

Spatial considerations and deliberations are prominent components in the artists' process. Through analysis of the object's scale in proportion to the viewer, the non-personal nature of the work increases. Scale dictates the relationship the viewer has with the art object. In order to avoid intimacy the scale and proportion often is larger than typically experienced.

While certain optical and sensory elements suggest Op, these elements in Minimalism are not based on illusion but rather the sensory perception activated by real structural and spatial relationships.

Certain characteristics of preceeding styles are apparent in the underlying objectives of the Minimalists. However, their synthesis of these elements and their blatant deemphasis of content and subject matter provide an overt and radical distinction between them and previous styles. By combining aspects of painting, sculpture, architecture and industrial manufacturing, they transversed two- and three-dimensional barriers and classifications. Art could no longer be described by media classifications, (i.e. painting or sculpture) but rather as the "art object." Within this terminology the autonomous and self-contained qualities of art were further espoused. Through the simplification of geometric form and the industrial "perfection" of its presentation, an ambiguous distinction developed between what was exclusively considered design and that which was art. As a result of this seeming ambiguity between design and art, the works were initially criticized. "Primary Structures," the first major group exhibition of these works, was held at the Jewish Museum in 1966. This exhibition demonstrated the unique spatial, structural and sculptural qualities of these works and dispelled much of the initial criticism.

Donald Judd, a critic of the apparent impasse occuring in painting and of the approaches and objectives of sculpture prior to Minimalism, executed his first works in 1963. Noted primarily for his unitary cube structures, Judd restricts both his materials and palette to industrial materials and pigments. Since 1966 his works have been produced primarily by industrial fabricators who work from his specifications. Judd utilizes both wall and floor in his environmental structuring and composition of space. Working either with one unit or a set of unitary structures placed in repetitive and sequential order, Judd isolates geometric form in a manner in which the object pushes, forces and defines the space which it inhabits, both internally and externally, ultimately declaring its perceptual dominance. The cube, square and rectangle are no longer parts of a whole, but the whole itself dictating and defining its own existence, presence and visual priorities.

The execution of works specifically for designated environments, as well as the uninhibited utilization of wall and floor space occur often in Minimalism. Sol LeWitt adheres to this practice in *Series A,* a 1967 installation at the John Weber Gallery in New York. Working with the grid, this piece encompasses the entire width of the floor space. This grid then acts, almost as a carpet, for dispersed, interconnected and open rectangles and squares which project three dimensionally from its surface into space.

Marvin Brown, while utilizing primary geometric structures and industrial materials common to the Minimalists, adds textured materials to the object's surface inducing sensuous and tactile qualities in the work. Geometric form in isolation is disturbed as the structure becomes the base or container for the additives. A contrasting interaction occurs within the works as the smooth and textured, the static and rhythmic co-exist. This co-existence in *Untitled 1976-1977*[22] subdues the prominance of the square as it is the base in which the folded screens rhythmically perform. The weaving of the screen and resulting shadows allude to depth and dimension as the screen vies for perceptual dominance.

Reminiscent of the field explorations of painters, *Untitled 1972* is dominated by textural fields of varying intensities as the rectangle acts as a frame in which the texture is confined.

Utilizing the grid, *Untitled Drawing, 1974* continues its prominance of textural effects created by varying the intensity and the gestural diagonal motion of the graphite on paper.

Borrowing from the structural and objectivity of the Minimalist and applying it to representation of recognizable subject matter, a new interest in realism and figural painting emerged. This New or ''Super'' Realism lacks the ironic, almost satiric, qualities inherent in Pop Art. Rather it presents an immaculately detailed copy of our own environment, often brutal and harsh in its truthfulness. Many of these New Realists work from the photograph rather than the actual object or subject. Although the final work appears to be a direct and impersonal translation of the subject matter, the artist can and does deal with various manipulative processes.

Although he does not use the photograph as the model for his paintings, Philip Pearlstein does utilize camera technique in his works. Bold and unidealized naked bodies pose in a straightforward, nonchalent manner amidst the intricate but homey patterns of living room rugs and sofas. Identities of the figures are anonymous because the models extend beyond the boundaries of the frame, thus cutting off their heads. The result is not unsimilar to a cropped photograph. Since the poses seem candid, with the nudes seemingly oblivious to their unclothes state, and the bodies are shown with all their imperfections, Pearlstein's work is simultaneously ugly in its extreme reality but exciting in an almost voyeuristic way.

Chuck Close uses photography as the integral instrument in his works of giant close-up facial portraits, rather than painting from the live model. By using a camera, Close is able to adjust focal points and can thereby manipulate the technical aspect of the art of photography to suit his own creative viewpoint. Instead of converting the three-dimensionality of the sitter's head to the flat canvas, Close works directly from the two-dimensional photograph. The resulting image is overblown and stark in its frankness. Every line, blemish and imperfection is seen and amplified. What initially appears as a literal translation of the subject, is seen on closer inspection more as an abstract rendering of surface areas and textures.

Although Manuel Hughes' technical facility and meticulous depictions of his subject matter could be categorized in the new realist mode, the artist feels more of a kinship with the surrealist and metaphysical tradition.

Having studied academic realism, for the last fifteen years Hughes has been exploring the tension between realism and abstraction. This pull of opposing forces is still apparent in his current paintings and drawings. Short, rounded metal strips or curved, white strips found on bleach con-

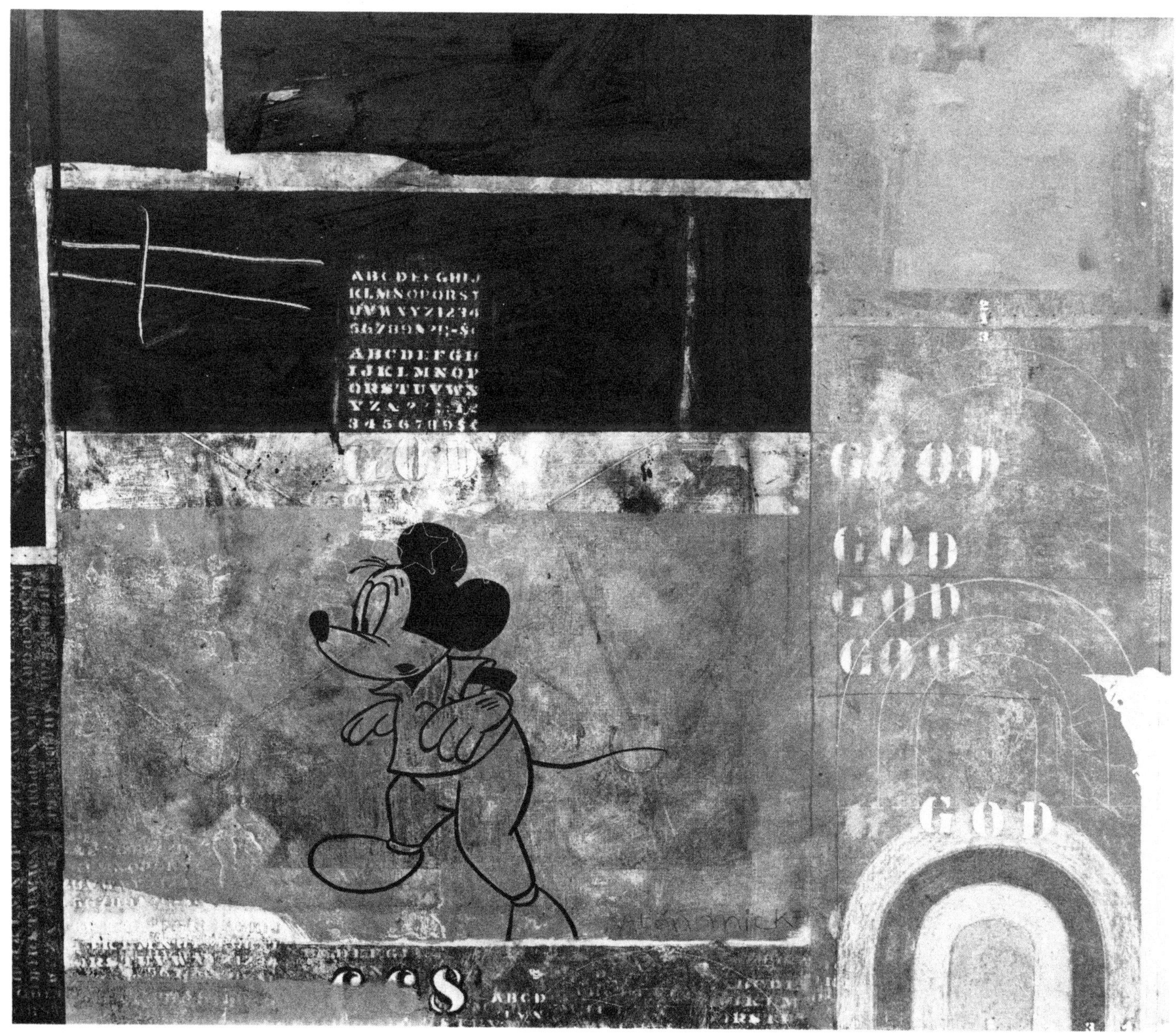

12. RAYMOND SAUNDERS. *Dr. Jesus. 1969*

tainers appear against a stark background broken up only by their shadows (fig. 14).

Hughes' studio is equipped with many bright, moveable spotlights. The artist arranges his composition, which he terms a still life, on a board and places the lamps at varying angles and levels. The multiplicity of shadows seems unnatural and surreal but, nevertheless, accurately depicts a precise duplication as a result of Hughes' manipulation of the lighting.

Because of the flexibility of Hughes' methods, both the strips and lighting effects, the artist is free to change or modify the compositional elements at all times. He is interested in order and balance, although asymmetry prevails, as well as the patterned effect of the shadows. Painterliness and gesture are avoided while minimalism in color and brush work is stressed. The space is open and the strips stand against a void as if alienated totally from their surroundings. The background space therefore acts not merely as a backdrop but more as the focal point to promote this feeling of alienation.

Since light and shadow exude an emotional force that exceeds other properties of the work, Hughes eliminates bright and distracting colors. His paintings are executed in subtle metallic and earth tones. This coolness enhances and enriches the metaphysical and spiritual quality of the work in which an unknown but powerful force seems to exist just beyond or underneath the surface.

Hughes' drawings are done in pastels on colored paper and also reflect a tonal softness in hue. The artist chose this medium for his drawings since pastels give a tactile, three-dimensional sense to the work and the strips seem to reach out from the surface to the viewer so that one feels that they can actually be removed from the paper.

Returning to automatism and the unconscious mind, a post-minimalist attitude occurred in the late 1960s. Termed Process Art[23] and primarily three-dimensional, the artists use physically non-substantive, limp and organic material causing a radical change in the qualities and properties commonly associated with sculpture.

These materials, utilized in their natural states, are usually contained, lumped, leaned, slumped or clumped in stacks, piles and drapings, or in a supportive structure. This accounts for the tactile, often sensuous, textural and referential qualities inherent in the works. The geometric and ordered presentation of the Minimalists was replaced by impermanent randomly placed amorphic form.

The use of the wall, floor and overall spatial considerations of the Minimalists was retained and expanded upon as these Process artists increased their freedom to penetrate environmental space and to create atmospheric conditions. The systematic rigidity of the Minimalists was altered, however, as the Process artists allowed the results of execution to determine the final character and nature of the object, no matter how happenstance.

With its emphasis on process, the art object was not restricted to physical and tangible objects. Perceptual and conceptual properties were illuminated and often dominated the visual characteristics of the works. Process became the subject matter, exposed by the automatism and natural properties of the material and process employed by the artists to arrive at the final art object or image.

Robert Morris moved from mixed-media sculptures and minimal objects to Process Art in the latter part of the 1960s. In his critical essays during this period he termed the art "anti-form" producing works which included audio as

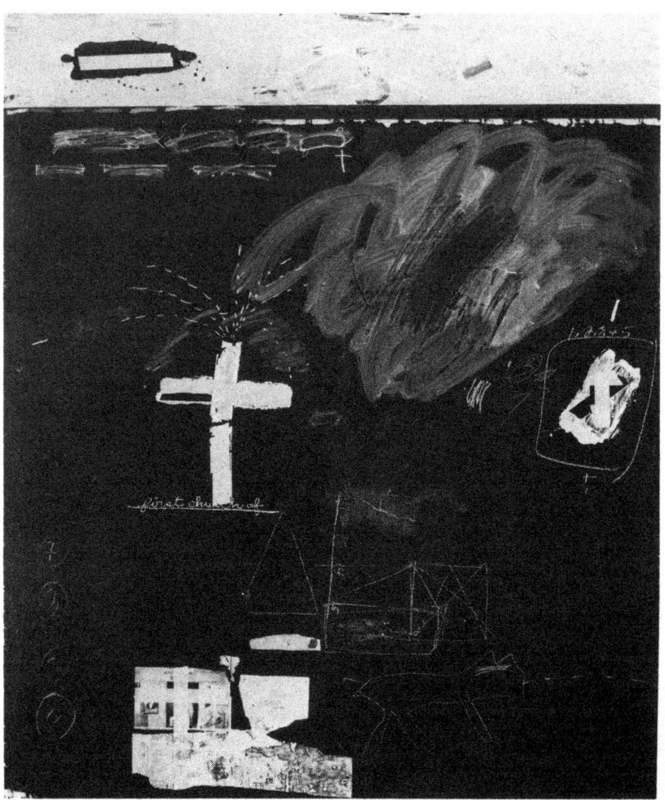

13. RAYMOND SAUNDERS. *1,2,3,4,5. 1974*

well as photographic components.

Further eliminating the spatial, material and environmental limitations to which the art object was traditionally confined, in the late 1960s Earthworks emerged produced by such practitioners as Robert Smithson, Robert Morris, Michael Heizer, Carl Andre and Richard Long. The focus on organic and natural material led to the direct use of natural phenomena. Initially artists brought this phenomena into the confines of the gallery. The expansive potential of this material, however, induced the artists to go beyond traditional exhibition procedures. Nature became art, its subject matter, material and content. "Instead of putting a work of art on some land, some land is put into the work of art."[24] Land excavations, shapes, patterns and rudimentary forms were pressed and pulled from natural landscapes.

Working two-dimensionally, John Dowell's works suggest a hybrid approach to process and method, and imply a synthesis occurring between the structural and systematic method of the Minimalists and the automatic, intuitive and unconscious process of Process Art. A subtle yet persistent visual dichotomy occurs as seemingly contrasting elements collaborate to produce the time and space fields of his prints, drawings, watercolors and paintings.

Initially, Dowell worked figurally and expressionistically in a manner reminiscent of Willem de Kooning and Franz Kline. By the mid 1960s, however, his interest in music ignited him with a concern for and interest in the visual presentation of time. Analyzing and mentally perceiving the qualities of music which allude to time and space, he developed a series of prints which utilized both fore- and background in an overall interplay of lyrical yet sporadic and spontaneous, movement. Biomorphic forms move freely and randomly in and out of broken color and shaped backgrounds, creating rhythmic movement and activity.

By 1967 Dowell increased the spatial areas by reducing the number of forms. An oval shape dominates the imagery of the picture plane, often in isolation or accented and enhanced by small and contained linear gestural movement. The oval floats in a volume of space *(Portrait of Bud, 1968)* suggesting a moment in time, an experience.

Meter, time and space become more dominant in the works of the early 1970s. Utilizing a grid system, Dowell executed a series which he termed "visual poems." These poems consist of hieroglyphs and calligraphic notations which lie on a field of linear and atmospheric color markings placed on a grid background. By reducing the area in which these notations inhabit, large areas of open grid provide the space which accompany meter and time in an overall composition of sustained and spontaneous visual activity.

During this period, his scores for music developed. Continuing his concern for the visual presentation of time in space, Dowell focused on the properties of time in sound. The space in between the sound in music was correlated with the space in between the visual marking. Structure as well as the spontaneity define his space and order providing lyrical, improvisational and intuitive character to his visual notations.

Dowell does not intend to interpret music, but rather transforms and translates the properties of music into visual perception. The basis of this transformation is his perception of audio structure. The marks and areas of color, therefore, become structural equivalents to the notes and spaces between the notes in musical scores. What results is a visual image not dependent on music for perception nor directly representational of a musical composition. Rather his visual sounds embody their own definitions which illuminate the common properties of both the visual and audio media.

This dual perception and equivalence allow Dowell's works to act as scores for musical compositions. Because they are primarily structural, the musical interpretation which occurs may vary as long as the structure is maintained. The very nature of the dichotomy which exists between order and disorder of the structure provides a basis and necessity for improvisation and freedom of interpretation. The time, space, meter, line and emotion (usually achieved through color contained in the markings) act as structural guides from which the musician can independently or collectively devise sound.

In *L.P. W.S., 1976* (fig. 15), this structure is contained within an atmospheric haze of blue which provokes a melancholic minor chord of moody emotion. An interfaced rectangle of linear notations provides the specific structure of sound as long duration and quick sporadic jutting, and at times, interlaced symbols blueprint its character.

Acting as a void in which the markings clarify its space, white dominates the ground of his canvases since 1972. The canvas texture, no matter the subtleties, becomes the haze in which structural notations are interspersed. In *To*

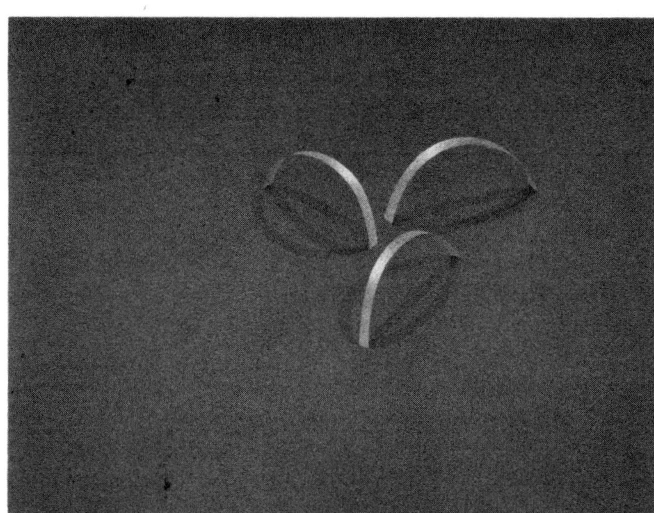

14. MANUEL HUGHES. *Thrice Light. 1976*

Dance Yesterday's Dreams, 1977 (pl. 8) these lyrical markings suggest a playfulness and up-tempo rhythm which is mysteriously subdued by the isolated nature of their placement and their suggested earth-toned mood.

Recently Dowell has begun plans for utilizing his visual structures of time and space as notations for dance movements.[25] Continuing his focus on exposing the structural commonality between all creative media, Dowell's art becomes the indefinite integral in which the creative process can emerge.

The concept "art" has traditionally relied on physical documentation which embody its philosophical and aesthetic principles for reaffirmation. The creative process has been the mechanism in which these principles are translated from concept, materials and process into visual perception. The art object acts as the tangible description of the "concept" art.

During the mid 1960s an art form emerged which repudiated this physical translation of the concept art and the premises which designated the visual form in which this concept would exist. Termed Conceptual, the artists involved have been primarily concerned with releasing concept to a perceptual autonomy not determined or restricted by physical properties.

In general, the term conceptual usually refers to post-minimalist abstraction. Specifically, however, it relates directly to works produced by artists who are primarily concerned with " . . . theoretical examination of the concept 'art' and the putting forth of concepts as art."[26]

Conceptual Art is an apparent and direct outgrowth of the methodical process and objective nature of the Minimalists, the unrestricted material and spatial explorations of the Process artists, coupled with the reactionary philosophy and challenge to traditional aesthetics of Duchamp. The Conceptualists radically alter traditional aesthetic formulas. The physical art object is no longer necessary since the art work becomes the intent, meaning, idea and objective of the artists. Art describes itself through concept and, thus, the need for physical affirmation or appearance ceases unless the object is used as the idea.

The Conceptualists work as prescribers of art rather than describers. The need for the critic is reduced since the artists, in this role, explain and define their intent through their art work. With this emphasis on verifying and systematizing intent, these works immediately become associated with philosophy and science.

Basic components in Conceptual art are idea, knowledge, documentation and relational properties existing between events, physical occurrences and conceptions. Language becomes the material and media in which the concept exists. Tedious analytical exposés involve either written or audio documentation. The artists often become the art work as they present their concept and intent through action or verbal proclamations, recorded and documented by audio and photographic media.

Analysis and philosophy are the primary content in the works of Adrian Piper, whether exposed through a written exposé, an action by the artist, or an art work which is the idea or intent. This emphasis on analysis is apparent in her work, *Three Models of Art Production Systems,* March 1970.[27] By devising a key of elements (I, C, P) she establishes three systems in which the key is transformed into a set of transitive equations.

In her recent works, Piper is concerned with analyzing the effects of political content in the work of art.

"The mental process of conceiving and refining an idea is very important because that is where all the creative work goes on. The physical process of realizing isn't that important, but it is very exciting to see how far one's ideas square with a possible reality, after all. (Presently) my feeling is that only by recognizing that one's choice to make (a certain kind of) art has political implications, and incorporating this knowledge itself into the art (we) choose to

make, can (we) be a politically responsible individual. Thus my primary objectives are: to convey significant political information; to stage a dialectic between the work (sometimes myself) and the viewer concerning the content of the work and its political implications; to explore the aesthetic defense mechanisms—i.e. the attitudes mentioned above—that seem to prevent the viewer from fully recognizing the reality of the particular content, but rather allow her/him to relegate this information to the 'realm of the aesthetic.'

"My most recent work has involved presenting political information obtained through the mass media in an art content, in a way designed to counteract the common tendency to focus on the formal properties of a work at the expense of its content. For example, my piece for the Paris Biennale, Art for the Artworld Surface Patter, *utilized newspaper clippings concerning the student riots in Cambodia and South Africa, Earthquakes in Turkey, martial law in Chile, etc. arranged in an arbitrary pattern and reproduced as wallpaper. Across the wallpaper is stenciled in red paint the words 'Not A Performance.' A taped monologue, intended as a satire of the above mentioned attitudes, accompanies the piece. It talks about how politics isn't art, why must we deal with political editorializing when seeking an aesthetic experience, we've already read about the latest world disasters in the* Times *so we don't need to repeat the experience in a gallery, art should deal with aesthetics and not with the world, etc., etc.*

"Communication between my work and the audience is intrinsically important to the success of the work. Its objective is complete social self-consciousness on the part of each member of the audience."[28]

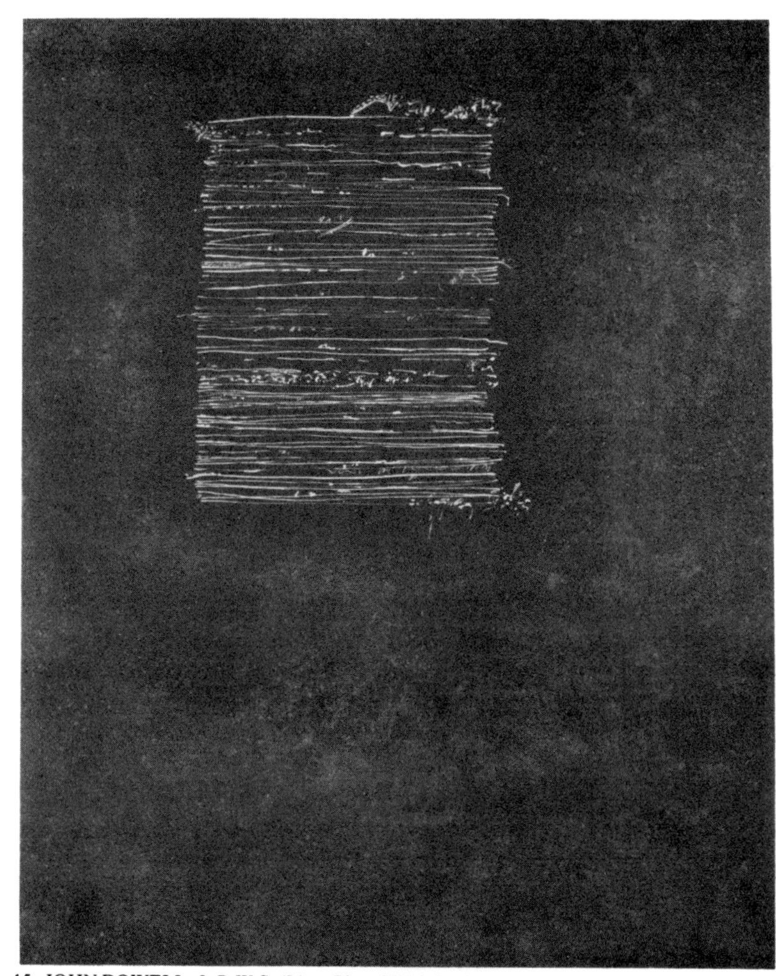

15. JOHN DOWELL. *L.P.W.S. (Lines Played With Soul). 1976*

CONTEXTURES

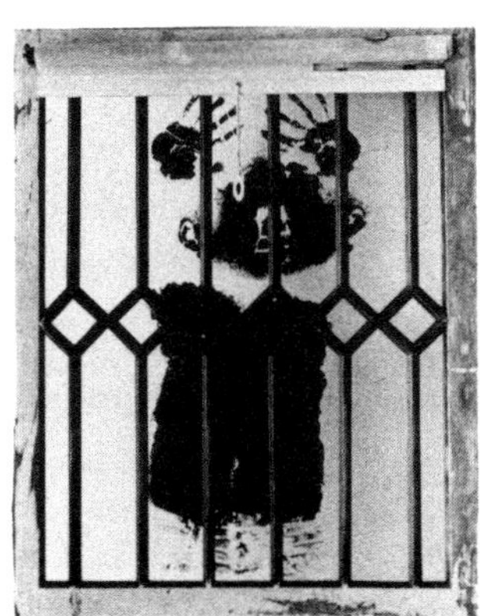

16. DAVID HAMMONS. *Black Boy's Window. (Detail). 1968*

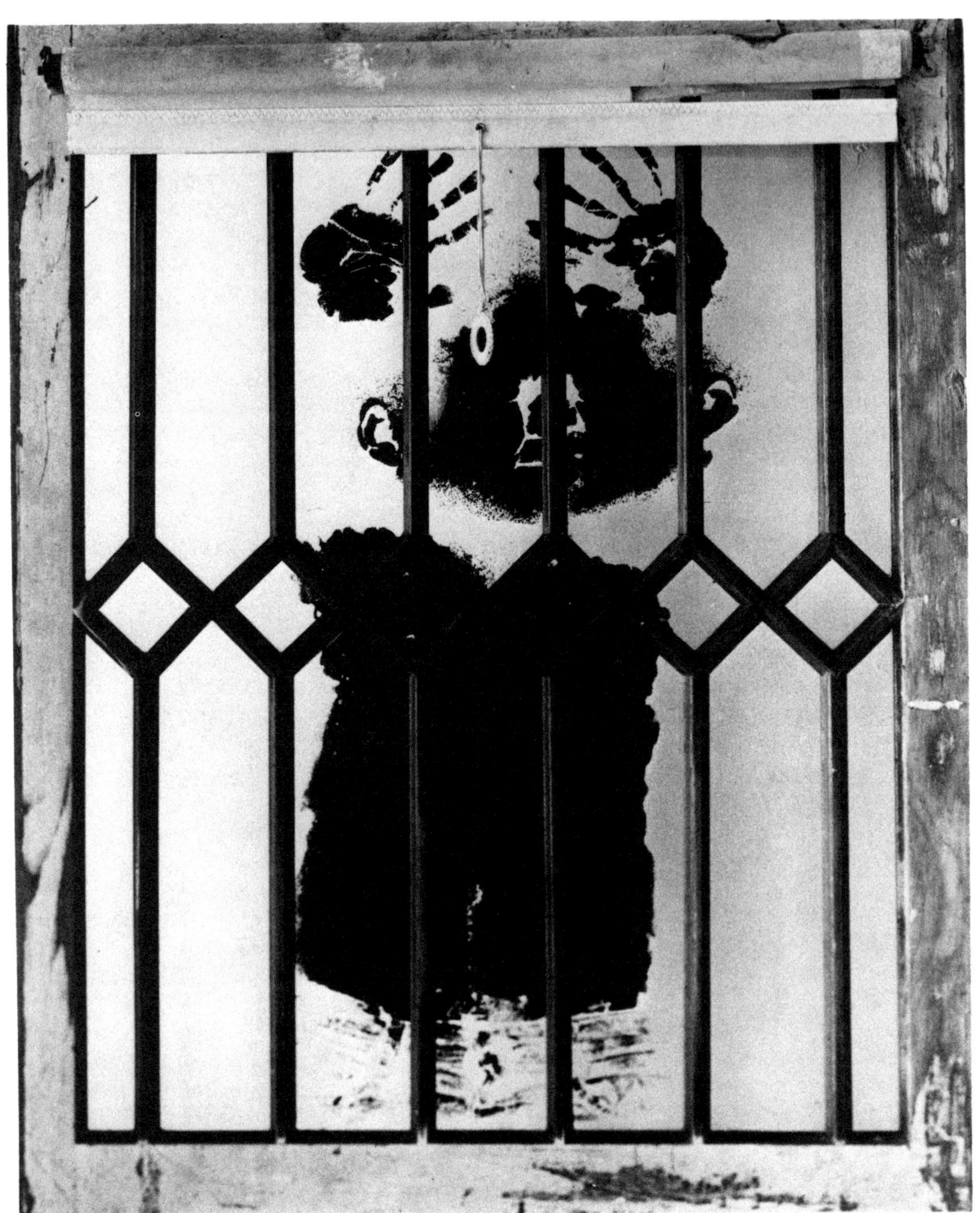

17. DAVID HAMMONS. *Black Boy's Window. 1968*

Developments in abstraction over the past seven years have invariably reflected further investigation of Dada, particularly Duchamp, and Surrealist references and/or premises and philosophies of styles developed since the mid 1940s. Thus the process, materials, artist and art object interchangeably become the prominant elements of content and intent.

Abstraction, since Abstract Expressionism, has consistently been involved in the isolation, reduction and illumination of the physical, perceptual and metaphysical properties which constitute reality. The nature of these pursuits has been primarily focused on finding and exposing these properties as they exist naturally and inherently within the confines of the art object. In doing so, the art becomes self-definitive ceasing to rely on or refer to external phenomena for definition. By isolating and separating its physical, perceptual and metaphysical properties, reducing its effect on and relation to external phenomena and maintaining its definition within the art object's confines, art is placed in a restricted context; its definition and, thus, reality are marginal.

In a radical departure from this method, process and approach to art, a notable development has been occurring since the early 1970s based not on direct derivative associations nor on a synthesis of the past. Termed Contextures, the artists involved in this movement, after determining and clarifying the inherent properties of art, go outside its margin in order to incorporate it within the context of external phenomena. It is through this process of clarifying and incorporating the contents of the margin that they define the context meaning and relationship between art and reality. Characteristically, the marginal elements will maintain their nature and integrity throughout this incorporation and, thus, define their specific selves. Simultaneously their contextural meaning will be exposed.

While common factors exist between the works of the artists involved, the nature of its development appears happenstance and can be noted on the East and West coasts, particularly in New York and Los Angeles. The artists work independently resulting in individually designed objectives. Relationships and similarities among them only become apparent through the cross-examination of these objectives, materials, process and ultimate visualization of their works.

Prominant factors which both distinguish and connect their works are primarily the role and position of art to reality, the role and position of the artist, and the process and the use of "remains" as the material in which the art objects are made.

Through an approach akin to modal logic,[29] the Contexturalists work from a method in which reality is perceived in two possible conditions: one, that it is reality; or two, that it is not reality. Through modality these statements of fact are considered merely as possibilities which may or may not be probable or actual. Rather than fixed, actual or certain, these statements become transient and only find clarity and definition through the contextural and transitive process used by these artists. In this sense, the artist acts as a medium in which the properties and conditions of reality are synthesized. Through this synthesis, the context whole of a given reality is presented.

The Contexturalists work primarily from their personal perceptions and accumulative experiences with internal and external phenomena. The artists' interest in the viewer and broader public becomes subordinate to their objective to define themselves, and to determine their own relative and context positions to reality.

The transitive process used by the Contexturalists consists of four elements: content, context, concept and definition. By maintaining the integrity of the individual properties an equation is established between them in which the properties of the first element are equal to the properties in each of the second, third and fourth elements. The characteristics of these properties will not be transformed or altered. The manner in which they are perceived during each elemental state tends to imply transformation. This implication, however, results from taking the actual marginal properties and placing them into context, thereby altering their perceptual meaning but not their physical characteristics.

As opposed to reduction and isolation the Contexturalists work from an additive method placing the content properties into context meaning. They go outside of the margin to complete the definition that exists within the art. Each individual property maintains its own distinction which, when incorporated in context, not only defines itself but also the environment in which it inhabits.

The use of " remains" as material is common throughout the works of these artists. The extent to which remains are used, however, varies. At times they are the dominant material and constitute the art object (Hammons) or they are incorporated with other objects and materials, often ready-mades and discards, in order to formulate the nature and characteristics of the art object (Williams). The types of remains which are used ranges from clothes dryer lint, smoke (fumage), sand and hair, to wax, grease, paper dots from hole punched paper and wood.

By definition, remains constitute the matter or substance left over from a primary action. Unlike a discard, which had a function or purpose that ceased to perform, or a ready-made which has an intended purpose and function which it still performs, the remain has no particular purpose or function, or a definition clarifying its intent. The nature and conditions of its existence are ephemeral. The properties of ready-mades and discards are stable. They are not flexible or meant to be transient.

Duchamp's *The Fountain* (a ready-made) when taken from its natural environment and placed into an art environment, physically retains its perceptual meaning. Conversely, it can be taken from the art environment and placed back into its natural environment without changing any of the properties which constitute its initial definition and reality. Its self-contained physical, perceptual and metaphysical properties will not alter in its presentation in either environment. However, the process of isolation and reduction, as well as its placement out of context in order to alter the manner in which it will be perceived, will completely transform its original intent, definition and function. The urinal, outside of its natural environ, ceases to be the urinal that exists within its own and natural reality. In an art context it is unable to perform its initial and primary function, intent, purpose or definition.

The transient properties of remains, however, allows them to be utilized within the transitive process of the Contexturalist without transformation, distortion or alteration in meaning. David Hammons' hair, when taken from its initial environment and incorporated within context, maintains its properties (physical, perceptual and metaphysical), and continues to perform its function. The hair, regardless of the environment and context in which it is placed, will maintain all its initial elements and properties. The external perception of the hair will not change. The context in which it is perceived may alter its meaning as opposed to the Dadaist process of isolation and alteration of the ready-made or discard which changes its physical, perceptual and metaphysical definition and reality. The meaning and reality of the remain will stay constant throughout its context incorporation.

An acknowledged element and consciousness shared by many of these artists has been music and dance. A spiritual quality, as well, is apparent in their works as they seek to involve, through context, the essence of reality. The works do not become symbols of the real or spiritual continuums, however, but rather become the transit in which these two elements co-exist. The nature of their work provokes sensory, psychological and visual perceptions.

Contextural elements have been apparent in the works of David Hammon; since the 1960s when he began exploring contemporary printing processes and abstracted figural forms. During this time he extensively experimented with various printing techniques involving and incorporating body imprints. Extracting all but the fundamental components of traditional printmaking and expanding on contemporary methods, he developed a body printing technique which directly utilizes the body as the printing plate. His process involves three stages as he works from the negative to the positive image. Oiling the areas of the body to be printed, he then presses them onto a surface. Through sifting powdered pigment, obtained from decomposed sticks of chalk (remains), these imprints are exposed.

Unlike methods commonly associated with body printing where the body marks a plate which is then used to transfer this marking onto a surface (Johns, Marisol, George Segal) or where the body is inked or painted, pulled, draped and rolled across a surface (Yves Klein) causing additional visual effects which distort the integrity of the actual impression of the body's surface, Hammons' method produces exact, accurate and undistorted impressions. His body prints maintain the integrity of the plate's surface producing imprinted replicas of body structure and texture.

Hammons' earliest body prints integrate social and political symbolism with distorted figural forms and textural compositions. Paradox, which he achieves through integrating commentary and satire into visual vignettes of seemingly contradictory imagery, becomes a significant element in the works created between 1967 and 1972. Initially these vignettes incorporated ready-mades and discards. Hammons, as well, translated the body print onto a silkscreen which was then used to transfer the imprint onto the final surface.

In *Black Boy's Window, 1968* (fig. 17), Hammons incorporated the body print within an actual window frame and panes. Transferring the initial imprint to silkscreen he disassembled the window, printing each pane separately. After the printing process had been completed he reassembled the window, panes and shade which could then be left up or pulled down by the viewer.

Hammons creates visual as well as structural tension within his compositions. Through the sequential placement of the six panes, the vertical perspective is accentuated by the central placement of the figure. By eliminating the arms, suggesting their presence only by the placement of hand prints on each side of the figure's head, the vertical pull becomes more prominant only to be contradicted by a decorative horizontal dissection. The embryonic stages of his technique is apparent as undefined textural areas inhibit the individual and distinct structural areas of the figure's imprint. Balance is achieved, however, by the emotive qualities of his images. A barred foreground and the elimination of the arms and lower torso of the body further accentuates the imprisonment of the figure.

Hammons has consistently worked with symbols. During this period the American flag is a recurrent theme; as the border and frame for *In Justice Case, 1970* to the body wrap for the female in *America the Beautiful, 1968.* Textural effects become more prominant as the hair and torso areas take on definable qualities.

Between 1969 and 1971, textural effects dominate the works. The symbol is removed and his considerations for space move from the geometric division of the picture plane to visual delineations which occur through textural transitions and juxtapositions. Hammons also relinquishes almost all allegiance to a literal presentation of the body's structure.

In *Close Your Eyes and See Black, 1970* (fig. 18) Hammons distorts the structure of the body making the parts compact and seemingly self-contained within the torso area of the figure. By controlling the amount and application of the powdered pigment, texture becomes a decisive element in defining the movement which occurs within the figure's confines.

During 1971 Hammons moved from paradox toward contextural definition. Focusing on social, political and symbolic connotations of actual objects, he began a series of works incorporating the spade shape which led him to a series of three-dimensional works using actual spades or shovels. Derogatory social connotations of the symbol are dispelled as the spade (cut, tied and chained) becomes a fetish-like apparition endowed with dramatic and spiritual overtones as in *Laughing Magic, 1973* (fig. 19).

Intrigued by the various possibilities of presenting the spade, Hammons developed a series of spade mysteries. Process works evolved involving the spade or its shape in a series of social and psychological dramas. From being killed by an automobile to being destroyed by its own image, these works return to paradox as they refer to racial, social and economical conditions.

Concurrently, Hammons continued his abstraction of the body prints. Employing aspects of his earlier assemblages, he superimposes the textural quality of the imprint onto the textural surfaces of collage material. In this series of works, areas of imprint are restricted to defining the interiors of the collage fragments. The spade shape is adjusted to a pyramidal form which is used as a decorative motif sequentially distributed throughout the background plane.

The body form was completely abstracted by the latter part of 1974. Eliminating collage, he restricted his surface to imprints defined by repetitive shapes and textures which he acquired from various types of cloth and found objects. To achieve this abstraction he alters his technique: first he oils and prints the shape which will define the external boundaries of the form; then he presses into and abstracts from this layer of pigment with body parts and found objects in order to define and abstract the internal areas *(Ragged Spirits, 1974)* (fig. 20).

Both stimulated by a growing interest in the work of Duchamp, as well as his concern that the creative process not be dictated by "need of money," and as a result of his use of found spades, Hammons moved away from a reliance on art materials. His objectives were constantly proclaimed as he sought to make art that " . . . no one will buy . . . outrageous art . . . it will make people think, think about themselves and what that means. You can't sell this . . . they won't buy this . . . old dirty bags, grease, bones, hair . . . it's about us, it's about me . . . it isn't negative . . . we should look at these images and see how positive they are, how strong, how powerful . . . our hair is positive . . . it's powerful, look what it can do. There's nothing negative about our images, it all depends on who is seeing it and we've been depending on someone else's sight . . . We need to look again and decide."[30]

Hammons' Bag Series consisting of found brown shopping bags, organic and manufactured grease, hair, rib bones and glitter emerged in 1975. Working from the

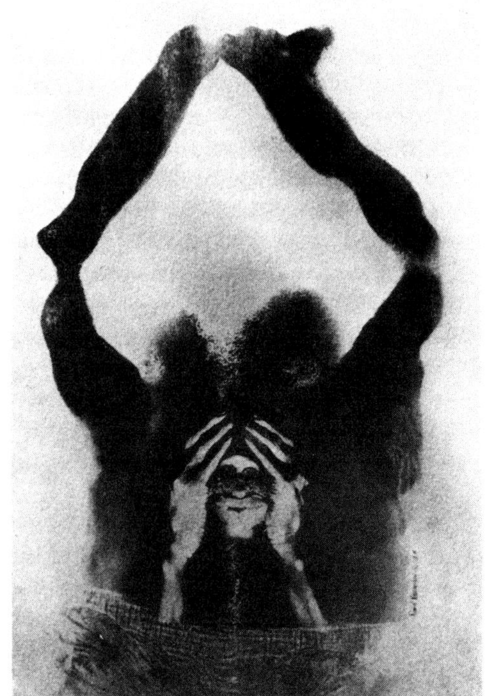

18. DAVID HAMMONS. *Close Your Eyes and See Black. 1970*

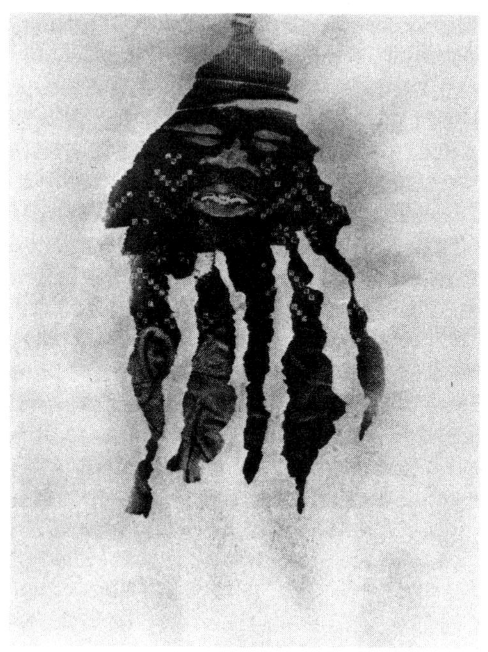

20. DAVID HAMMONS. *Ragged Spirits. 1974*

natural folds and crevices of the bags he developed the line and form compositions of these works. Attaching bag to bag, Hammons is able to construct horizontal and vertical movement by gradually changing the placement of one bag onto another. In *Untitled, 1976-77* (fig. 21), a wing-like form is projected on both sides of the vertical hair band which acts as the central axis. Resembling an open fan, the movement and direction of these undulating forms are emphasized by the paper's folds creased in a manner which allows them to jut from the surface creating a shadowy depth. Hammons stains the surface of the paper using thick and thin grease. Once the initial layer of grease is applied he rubs it into and out of the paper's surface creating stain variations. This accomplished, Hammons changes the type of grease. Again, rubbing into and out of the paper he is able to vary the staining effect and alter the surface complexion. Additional layers of grease are applied in order to provide textural build-up and variation. These areas are generally utilized to emphasize or de-emphasize the contrast between the light, dark and shadowed areas. Color is introduced by attaching glitter to the outer edges of the fans. Maintaining his pyramidal and triangular forms, these color areas assist in accentuating the movement of the outer edges and provide contrasts to the subtle stain patterns and coloration of the bags.

In many of these bags Hammons attaches the remains of barbecue rib bones. Glitter was sprinkled upon these uncleaned and naturally decaying attachments, and they were then tied to the outer edges of the bags in order to accentuate horizontal or vertical movement.

Intrigued by the effects of hair when incorporated within the Bag Series, Hammons began his Hair Series in 1976. His first work incorporated hair threaded wires with a Yoruba mask which was suspended from the ceiling and adorned with a gown of plastic. The hair-wire acted as a floor environment which enclosed the fetish. In subsequent works the hair was attached to found objects *(Murray's Can, 1976)* or placed behind glass in frames. These framed works primarily focused on the textural properties and compositional potentials of hair. Sifting coarse hair through a strainer, Hammons created a background of fine bits which were superimposed with curly locks and delineated with straight strands. These confined hair works were then freed, strung on rubber bands and stretched to scales of ten feet in length. Attaching and stretching rubber band to rubber band, Hammons developed wall drawings of lyrical and staccato movement. Jutting up, jutting down, dissecting horizontal and vertical planes, these seemingly suspended balls of hair perceptually intrigue and deceive as they allude to ephemeral motion while statically contained.

Through further investigation of the properties of hair, Hammons found that the sifted hair, when placed in a mold, could provide its own support. A series of hair pyramids was developed. Each individual and unified pyramid is imbued with its own distinctive textural and tonal qualities as in *Untitled, 1976* (fig. 22). Placing these pyramids on the floor, Hammons arranges them in a combination of open and closed patterns. An interest in pattern continues in the hair works as he uses the sifted hair as stuffings for holes in found metal and screens. These works generally consist of six to ten quilt-like components, and are often reminiscent of the geometric compositions found in African textile designs. Later, Hammons combines the hair threaded wires and screens with large forms of unsifted bodies of hair and barbershop debris, achieving a contrast between the patterned, linear and the undistinguishable.

In 1977, Hammons returns to the hair threaded wires, but now frees them from any attachments and allows their form and interaction to determine their line, movement and compositional structure. No longer confined, they create environments of lyrical, staccato and, at times, seemingly sporadic energy. In *Untitled, 1977* (fig. 23) each individual wire maintains its own perceptible characteristics and distinctions. In groups, they physically narrate their environment in a manner which often taunts the viewer into acknowledgement and interaction. This physicality is enhanced further by their organic, tactile and sensuous nature.

Untitled, 1977 (fig. 24) breaks from all restraint, distributing energy across the wall as the wires appear to grow, crawl and multiply while continuing the elusive and perceptual deception noted in the Rubber Band Series.

In *Untitled, 1977* Hammons physically confines the hairwires between the intersection of two walls. Almost in defiance of this restraint, the wires disseminate an energetic activity through their bending, pulling and interweaving creating a nervous tension and agitation. In this work, Hammons returns to his concern for the triangular-pyramidal form which he emphasizes by enclosing the right angles with hair wires.

Working with space, Hammons has maintained his concern for creating environmental and atmospheric conditions which provoke, engulf and contain the viewer. The nature of these works repel and intrigue, include and exclude participation from the viewer. The nature of this participation is based purely on the viewer's perspective and willingness to be included within the contextural composition and presence of the work.

Hammons continues his use of images, symbols and materials responding to a variety of attitudes and conceptions, often contradictory, which he then incorporates into his interweavings of the physical, perceptual and metaphysical properties of the internal reality of the art object and the external reality of experience. This contextural process allows him to assert and define his relative position to art and reality.

Hammons' interest in the viewer has been one wherein the conditions of their reaction and response is predicated on an environment in which contradiction and his contextural ' 'truth'' coexist. With no assistance, the viewer is left to decipher the distinctions.

Hammons' placement of the art on the ceiling in order to make "people look up,"[31] thus jolting their natural and usual position and relationship to the art object, occurred to him in the early 1970s which he conceptualized in *Gray Skies Over Harlem, 1977* (pl. 9). This environmental piece incorporates objects and materials from egg shells to tea bags and roaches with colored wire and hair. He alters the position and perspective of the viewer by placing the work on the ceiling subordinating the viewer to the object. This archeological-like icon continues to exude nervous and sporadic energy, dissecting the meaning and content of each object, collectively providing contrasts, conflicts and similarities through which his definitions and reality are proclaimed.

Tension, environment, architecture, atmosphere and emotion are prominant elements in the anthropomorphic structures of Senga Nengudi.[32] Working with nylon mesh and sand, she twists, pulls, intertwines and sags her material into sensuous and sensual emotive formations.

Nengudi's work during the latter part of the 1960s and early 1970s consisted of water-filled vinyl forms. Folded and twisted these self-contained transparent and physically limp structures were pushed into long, thin rectangular shapes. By adding color to the water (which was heat-sealed into the vinyl), Nengudi was able to juxtapose color

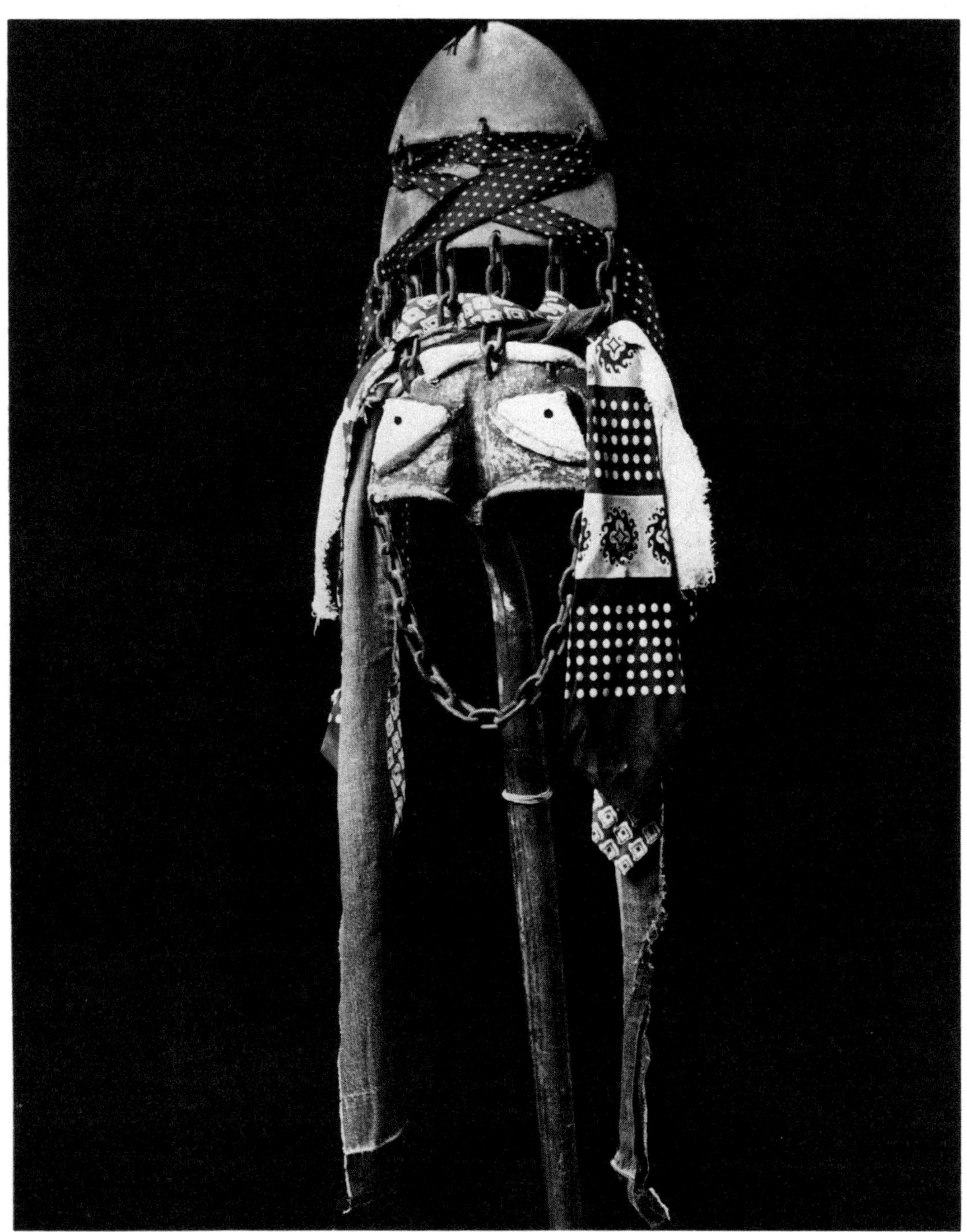

19. DAVID HAMMONS. *Laughing Magic. 1973*

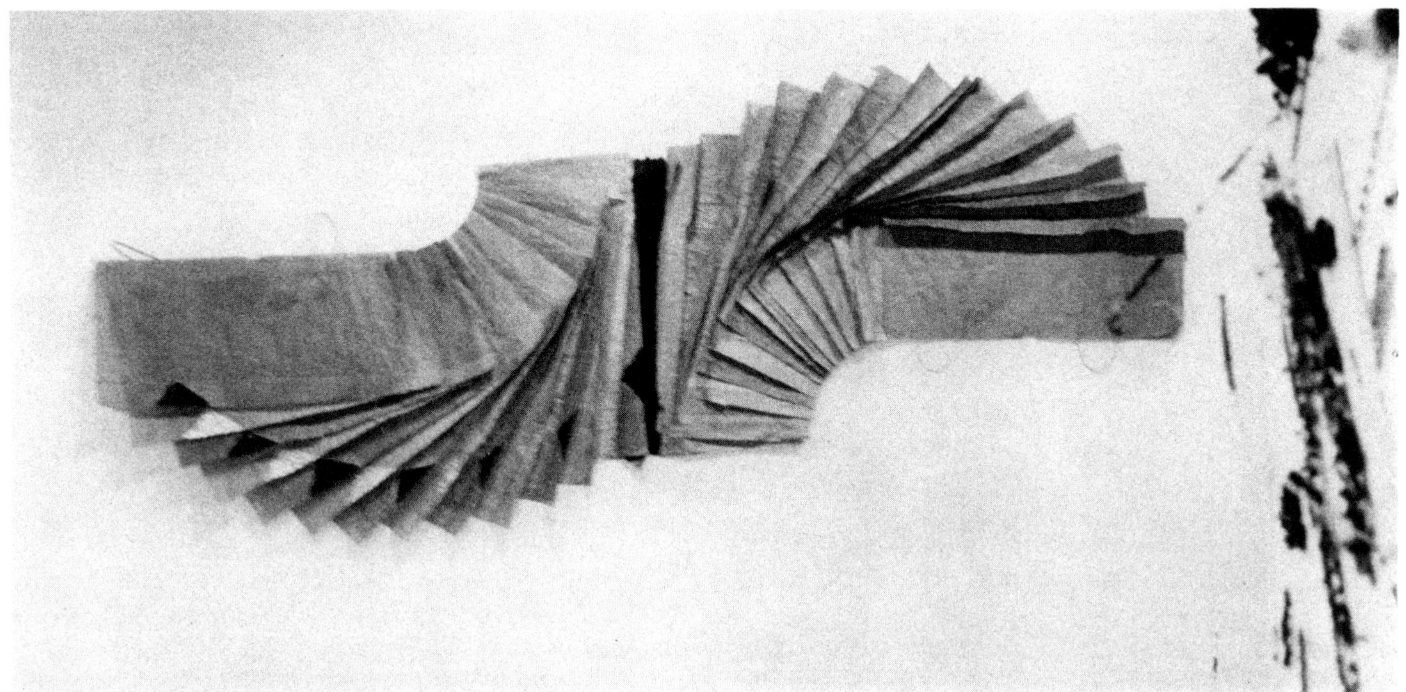

21. DAVID HAMMONS. *Untitled. 1976*

and form into layers of visually penetrable mass. Tension and flexibility were obtained through the varying distribution of water throughout the plastic, holding it in place by the folds and twist of the material and the weight of the water. These skin-like folded forms were often draped over ropes and twisted into figural distortions.

From the early to mid 1970s Nengudi experimented extensively with a variety of materials in order to decipher the qualities and properties which would be necessary to achieve maximum flexibility and elasticity. During this time Nengudi developed a series of works with rope and flag material. By tying these outdoors, the wind became an additional element in the works. Therefore, varied and unexpected undulating waves and movements occur as the air current interacts with the pliable forms, imposing a natural dimension into the work.

Nengudi had begun working with nylon in 1975 and in 1976 her nylon mesh and sand works emerged. One of her primary concerns has been the immediate impact of emotional, rather than intellectual, experience. With a background in dance, she seemingly choreographs the object's movement by the tense and abstracted interweavings of emotional, intellectual and social or human experience. Lyrical movement is embodied within the stretched and pulled linear extensions and appendages of the object's central axis.

Her initial works were self-contained, and the nylon stretch and extension were minimal. Distortion of the nylon's naturally limp condition was achieved through tying and knotting. In general, these works rely on the incorporation of ready-mades and discards as the foundation from which they will protrude, surround or extend.

In *Inside/Outside—Winter, 1977* (fig. 25), rubber, foam and sand act as determinants for the object's form. By placing the nylon mesh over horseshoe-shaped foam both covered with rubber tubing, and creating surface and textural interplays of contrasts from the cool, smooth and slick surface of the rubber to the grainy, warm and sensuous surface of the nylon, she is able to achieve subtle to sharp color and textural variations. Patterned stockings are exposed and emphasized as their stretch by the sand illuminates the threading.

The works increase their organic and sensual feel by stretching and knotting which allows the sand to fill in-

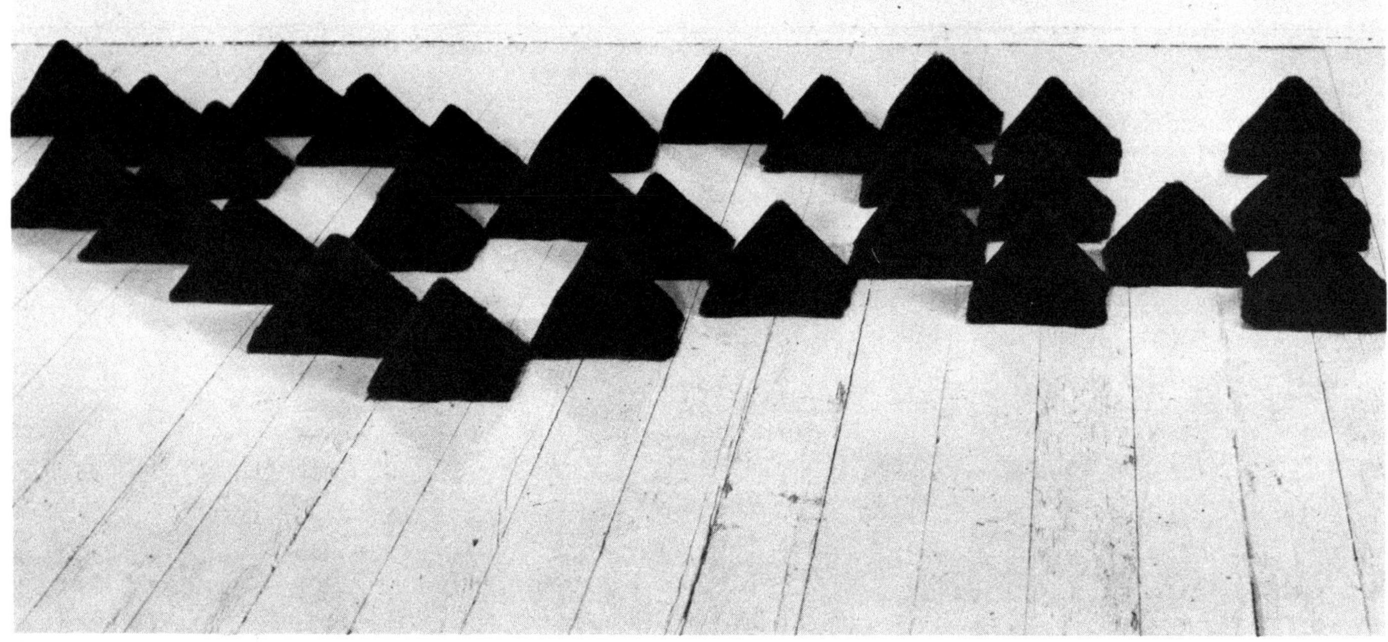

22. DAVID HAMMONS. *Untitled. 1976*

dividual pockets. Suggesting human organs these sand-filled pockets awaken and provoke the viewer's tactile sense since he/she is encouraged to poke and to squeeze, assisting the slow oozing of the sand from the nylon's pores.

While maintaining her incorporation of found objects and debris, Nengudi releases the nylon from its dependence on a foundation of support in *Chant—Winter, 1977* (fig. 26). The nylon becomes self-supporting. Stretching the waistband by one foot, Nengudi allows the nylon to define its form from its own natural folds and stretch. The waistband and pelvis extension act as the central axis. Tension is reduced and limited to the knotting of two nylons in what might constitute the focal point of the work in the upper center. Contrast is achieved through a fetish-like neckpiece which extends from the suspended waistband, and forms a horizontal dissection immediately below the knotted focal point. The rips, runs and tears are naturally exposed enhancing the subtle textural qualities of this piece. In contradiction, the piece exists in a relaxed suspension with the tension created through the stretched waistband support and central knot.

Nengudi works in a figural motif which is abstracted beyond specific visual references, but achieved through gesture, movement and an imagery indicative of body parts and structures. "I am working with nylon mesh because it relates to the elasticity of the human body. From tender, tight beginnings to sagging and . . . The body can only stand so much push and pull until it gives way, never to resume its original shape. After giving birth to my own son, I thought of black wet nurses suckling child after child —their own as well as those of others—until their breasts rested upon their knees,.their energies drained . . . My works are abstracted reflections of used bodies, visual images that serve my aesthetic decisions as well as my ideas."[33]

The tension and the strain, the sagging and the pull become prominant elements in *R.S.V.P. XIII,* March, 1977 (fig. 27). Reintroducing sand, Nengudi extends the nylon seemingly beyond its physical endurance by attaching it to the ceiling and wall from three points. This triangular formation acts as the boundary in which the central axis is developed. Incorporating sand into the dangling mesh the vertical pull is further accentuated. Tension exists within the stretched and attached elements as well as in those which hang loosely from the axis. Color, hue and textural variations persist as Nengudi continues to vary the type of nylon which is incorporated within the piece. The sagging pockets begin to taunt the viewer's sensibility since they resemble breasts or testicles which have been stretched to a state of anguish. The environmental and atmospheric nature of this piece engulfs the viewer, challenging response and participation while seducing the viewer through its tactile and sensual qualities.

Nengudi relaxes the tension in *Swing Low,* Spring, 1977 (fig. 28). Maintaining the triangular-pyramidal form she lessens the stretch of the nylon allowing areas to droop. In an almost suspended animated pull, the nylon is supported from the ceiling. A foreground horizontal band is created through two perpendicular nylon strips which are perceptually stablized by a lower horizontal fold and two sagging pockets of sand. The slight curvature from the two strips and the triangular pointed "head" alludes to a lyrical and almost demonic display of mischief.

In *Insides Out, 1977* (fig. 29) a tight-knotted tense disturbance is created through the utilization of the limited spatial area between the boundaries in a series of repetitive knots. Again, applying a discard as the hanging support for the piece, she concentrates the areas with varying pockets of sand and knots which tangle and squeeze. The dominating vertical emphasis stresses the tight and discomforted confinements since each contained element appears to struggle for unentanglement.

In *I, 1977* (fig. 30 & 31) Nengudi returns to her overall use of environmental space. The nylon and sand pockets act as testicles and breasts, stretched, pulled, suspended and rested expanding their tension from a repetitive series of attachments to the surrounding walls. The sensual, sensuous and tactile elements prevail as the atmosphere surrounds the viewer in a provocative seduction of his/her senses. Nengudi's concern for architecture becomes illuminated as the work defines arcs, corners and crevices accentuated by its confines.

Environmental divisions of space and form are apparent in *Internal I and II* (fig. 32 & 33). Extending the stretch and increasing the number of attachments to the wall, a lyrical and suspended form is achieved. Eliminating the sand, this work is purely defined by the stretch and pull of the nylon against the wall.

Symbolic imagery is implied more through the character and formation of form than through the nature of the materials and the incorporation of objects which have socio-sexual-political connotations in her context. Unlike Hammons, however, her iconography is more subdued, avoiding or subjugating the intellectual in order to evoke emotion and experience into concrete and prominent elements of definition and reality.

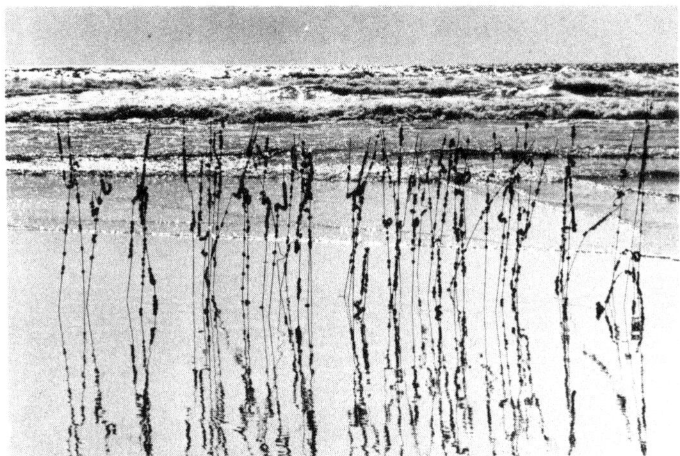
23. DAVID HAMMONS. *Untitled. 1977*

A bifurcation of natural and technological phenomena occurs in the works of Susan Fitzsimmons through her use of lucite and organic material in three-dimensional wall reliefs and sculptures. By equalizing the intellectual, scientific, and personal observation and interpretation she contexturalizes the elements of natural and man-made substances into co-equal physical states which share a commonality in their evolutionary process, and metaphysical conditions in modern society. Placing scientific and technological procedure into context with organic and natural phenomena, she creates a subtle yet poignant commentary on man's alienation to his/her natural and material environs. Her works address this alienation by combining the inherent properties existing within both realms into compatible and coexisting conditions, distinctively and collectively exposing the spiritual and material essence of modern existence. This exposure is rendered transparent as the process and properties of both realms are intertwined into methodical and stochastic relationships which allude to the past and present, and provide concrete indications of the future. Thus a mental methodology coincides with

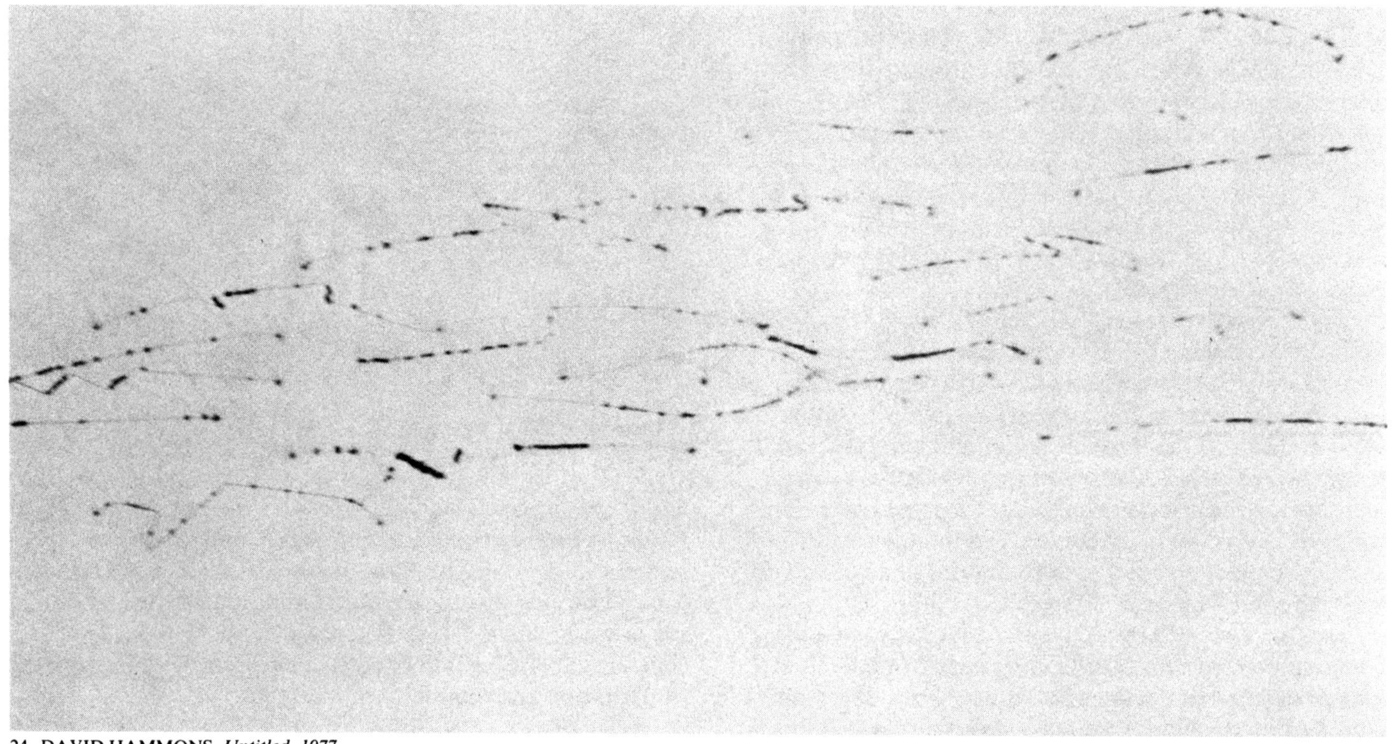

24. DAVID HAMMONS. *Untitled. 1977*

the contextural transitive process by conducting the predictability of the future through the existence of past and present facts. "If you are able to observe carefully, like an old lover noticing some new trait that was overlooked because of the dulling effects of habituation then it will grant you the chance to see things you haven't seen before. It will freeze transparent relationships in time and space."[34]

Fitzsimmons' works become models and systems which she examines intellectually. Gathering information, she synthesizes the properties and characteristics of this information into untransformed states of factual data.

In 1975 Fitzsimmons developed a hypothesis and formula, "New Arrangements Through Creative Work,"[35] in which a number of lucite works were developed from a process delineated into categories A through H. Using the method of modeling she was able to ". . . identify principle energy flow pathways . . ."[36] existing from the initial concept and energy source (artist) through to the final art object (The Surviving Information Series). Her method allowed for control and happenstance where random and arbitrary choice and systematic choice integrate to form the final object. While adhering to established technological formulas for producing lucite, Fitzsimmons altered and rearranged these processes which led to technical and manufacturing innovations with the material.

Fitzsimmons feels that the process of making lucite is similar to the process of photosynthesis. Lucite is unpredictable as are systems of nature. The material provides the necessary characteristics to represent a model, and lends itself to visual descriptions and exposure of the process. The natural substances of lucite also provide the connections between natural and material phenomena since the petrochemical component is derived from organic molecules. With the technical photosynthesizing of the material providing the original energy input, the evolutionary element and energy source are apparent when joined with an organic base.

During 1975 and 1976, Fitzsimmons used geometric cubes and prisms to provide her with her technical renderings. The transparency is treated with and without color as

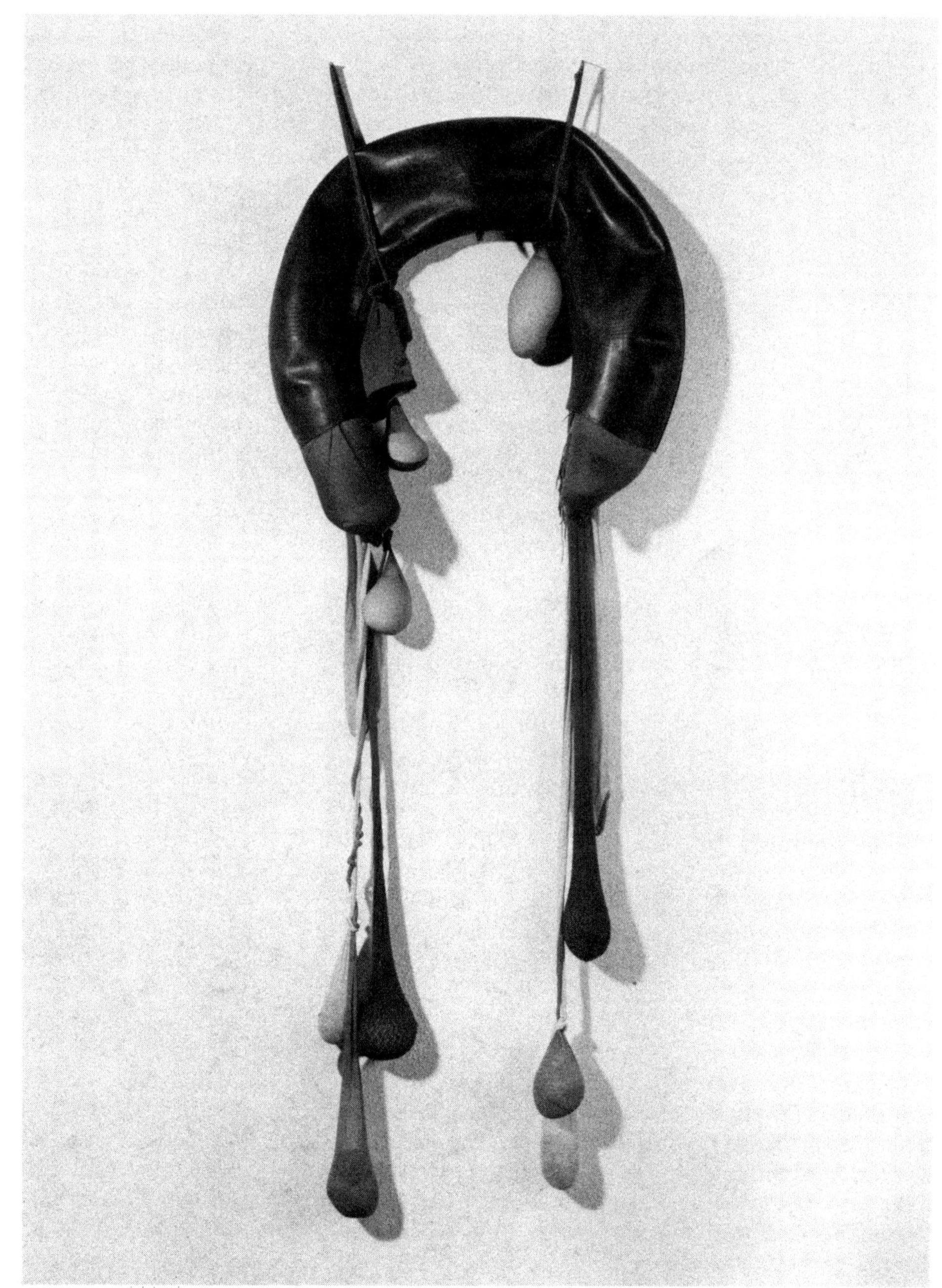

25. SENGA NENGUDI. *Inside/Outside. 1977*

texture and structure dominate the factual information of each work. By varying the process she is able to translate lucite into hazes created by deviating from traditional milling techniques which constitute the depth and level of transparent visibility. Her approach to color is similar to painting since it creates color fields of varying hue intensities. Often the variation and distinction will fuse within the prisms to create a solid color as in *All These Colors Make Brown, 1976.*

After technical experimentation with the material Fitzsimmons moved to her biform works incorporating manufactured and natural materials. Basing a series of works on the four seasons of the year, she analyzed the characteristics and properties of water occuring in all four conditions. Her selection of natural materials, particularly wood, becomes a process of both intent and happenstance. Initially her "imagination knows and recognizes."[37] A dialogue occurs between the wood and her concept in which the wood tells her what to do and she then dictates what the wood will do. After selection, the "plastic surgery" begins. Controlling the flow-formation of the lucite, unfinished, rough, smooth and sustained liquid are contained within transparent confines. The process is one of struggle, control and chance as she manipulates the process and method of forming the lucite and joining the wood.

In *Water—Summer, 1977* (fig. 34) the lucite is held between two vertical wood bands and introduced to a variety of natural debris and remains. The textural flow of the lucite is unrestricted resembling the flow of water; waves, streams, vibrations. In *Water—Fall, 1977* (fig. 35) the natural conditions of the wood interact with reds and browns contained within the lucite. Her use of joints to hold the structure upright is introduced in these works. Balanced, the works stand independently without need of nailing or cementing the parts into place.

In *Stick-Caught Cube, 1977* (fig. 36) the dichotomy between technology and organic reverberates as the lucite's surface is rendered smooth. The internal area of the lucite is allowed to flow in textural formations which directly relate to the surface of the sustaining wood. The effects of the prism are continued as the reflection and juxtaposition of the suspended wood-stick and lucite create varying reflections depending on the perspectives from which it is viewed.

A conscious examination occurs as the viewer is confronted with the dichotomy of his environ enabling him/her to dissect and decipher his/her relative position to the natural and material phenomenon. More importantly, man's alienation to his environment is challenged as the properties between the two become interrelated providing a balance in future meanlng and significance.

"My work is not about sculpture using a certain material, it is about the process of change described in my model. It is peripherally related to taking technologies that confront us, and better using them as tools for communication."[38]

The biform works of Gini Hamilton consist primarily of hard and soft, pliable and restraining, and repelling and absorbing relationships between materials. Her objects are composed of various types of cloth, steel and threads which are used to bind the soft and hard substances into three-dimensional units, creating structural and compositional devices that accentuate or subdue their natural characteristics. Thus, through pulling, stuffing, knotting and binding she obtains a restrained and sustained suspension of the cloth perceptually contradicting its naturally pliable and limp qualities. Cotton, lace and string take on visual characteristics resembling the weight, solidity and depth of traditional sculptural material. These cloth-bound forms are generally attached to the upper portion of a steel band. The nature of their attachment and binding allude to a dimension of weight, accentuated by leaning the steel on a supporting wall. The physical properties of steel are subdued as the cloth forms appear too heavy for the steel to support on its own. While the natural properties and qualities of these materials have not been altered the perceptual reversal which occurs jars any preconceptions of soft and hard, strong and weak into a reconsideration of physical facts and information. It is through the context in which these materials have been combined that this perceptual reversal of their properties and qualities occurs. Their clarification and definition, as well, are physically and essentially reversed by their contextural interrelations.

Underlying sexual connotations are apparent as the materials relate to stereotypical masculine and feminine traits. While tied, bound and knotted these soft, rounded and sensuous "cloth-females" push, force and pertrude through tensions and confinement taking on strong and dominant masculine characteristics.

The wall and floor act as foundations or supports for Hamilton's works. Her utilization of pull, stretch, stuffing and knotting is similar to that of Nengudi although Hamil-

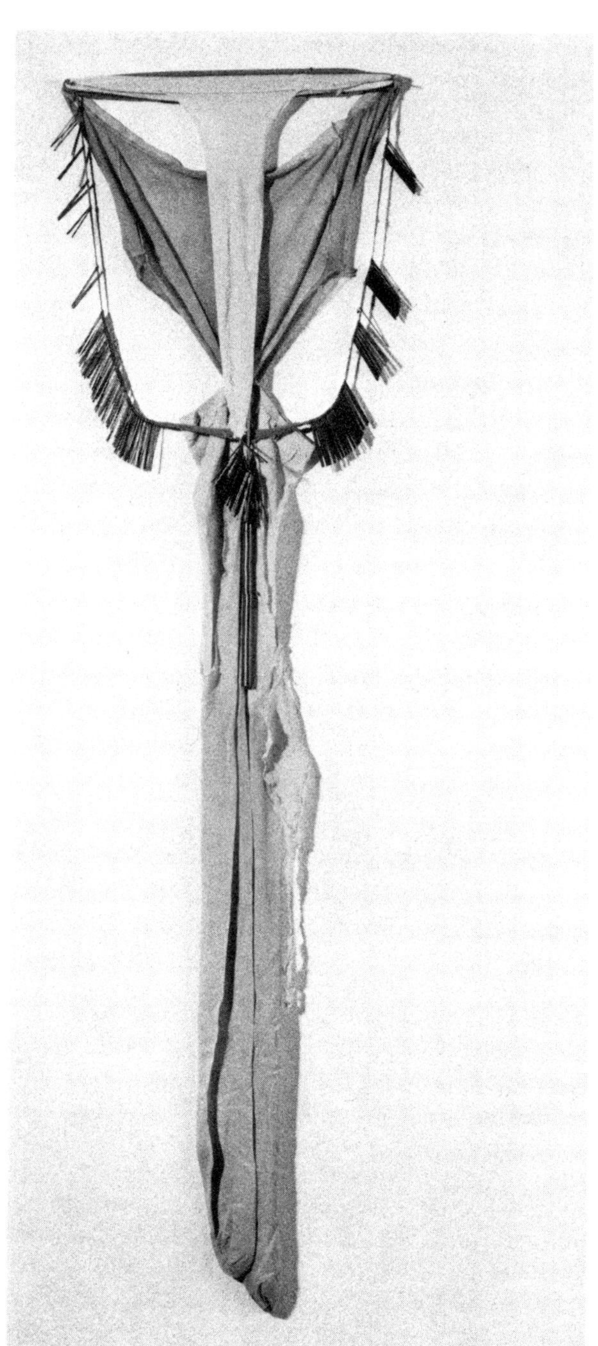

26. SENGA NENGUDI. *Chant. 1977*

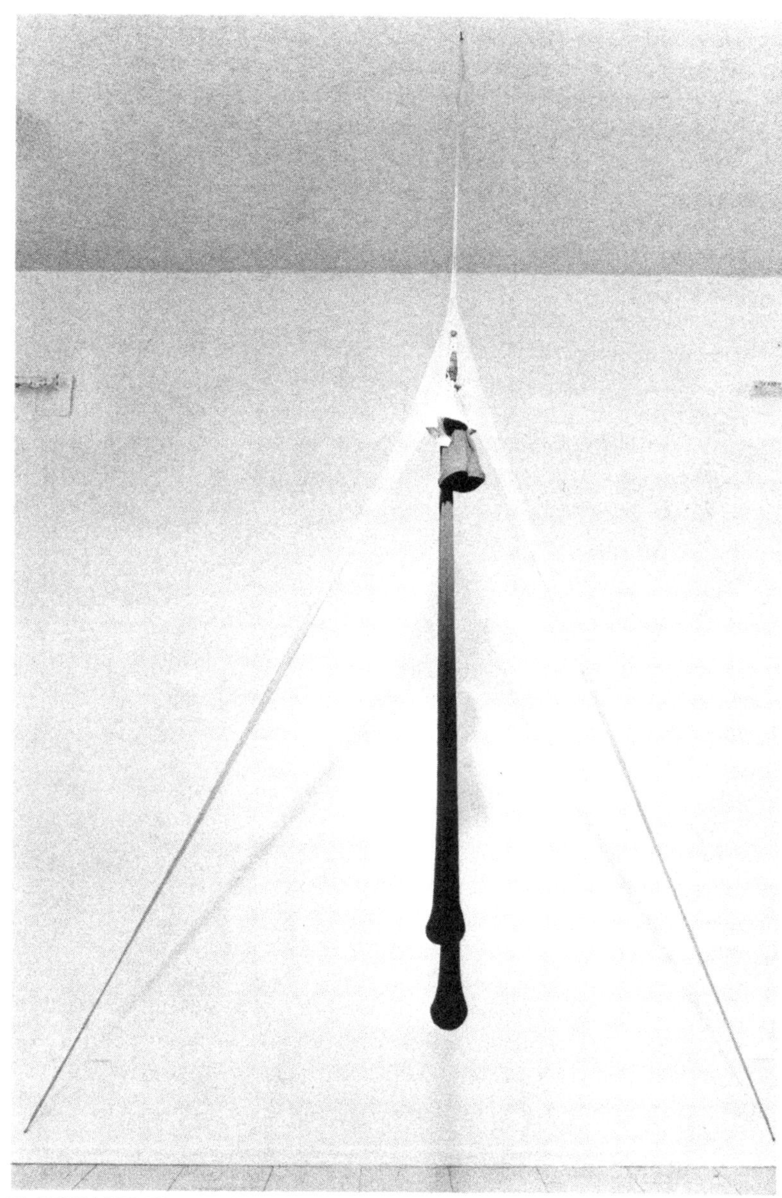

27. SENGA NENGUDI. *R.S.V.P. XIII. 1977*

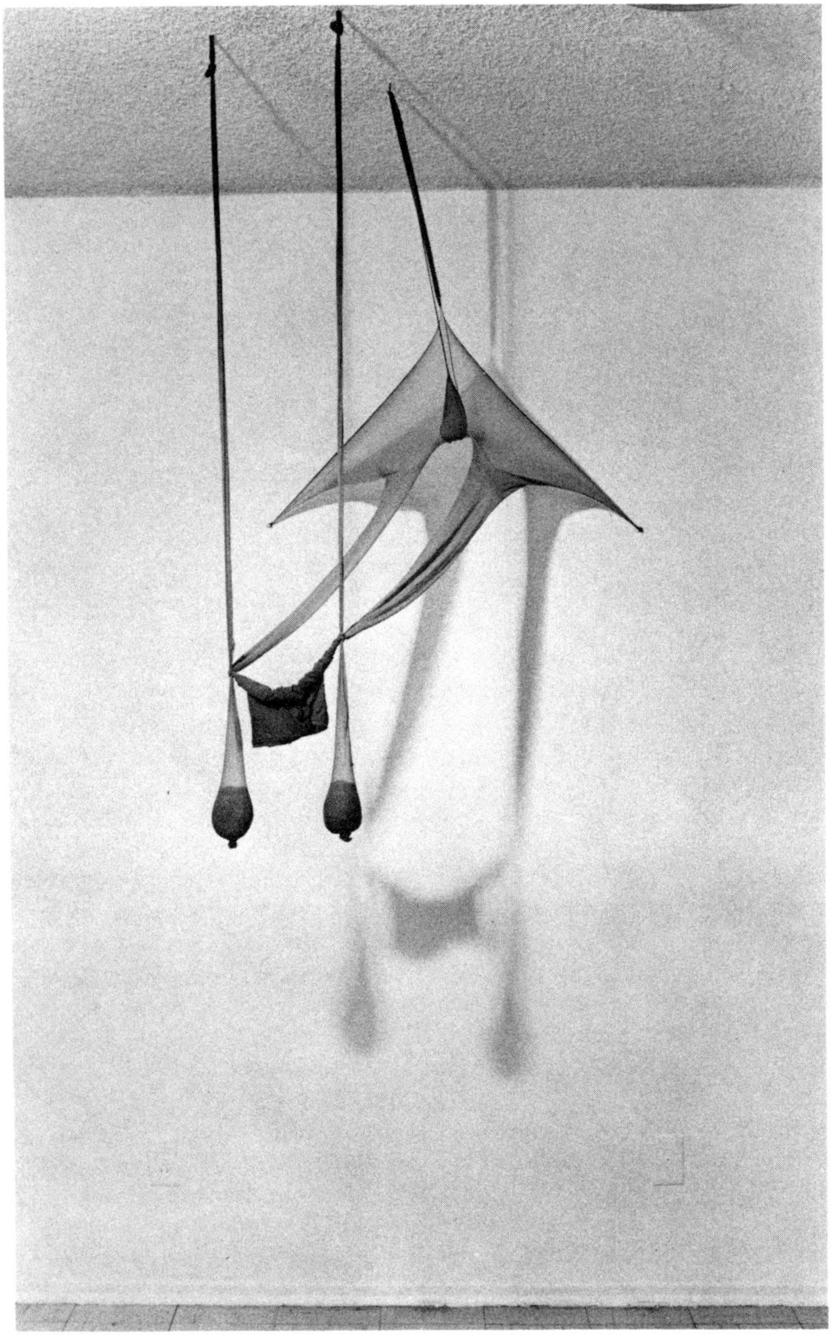

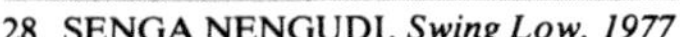

28. SENGA NENGUDI. *Swing Low. 1977*

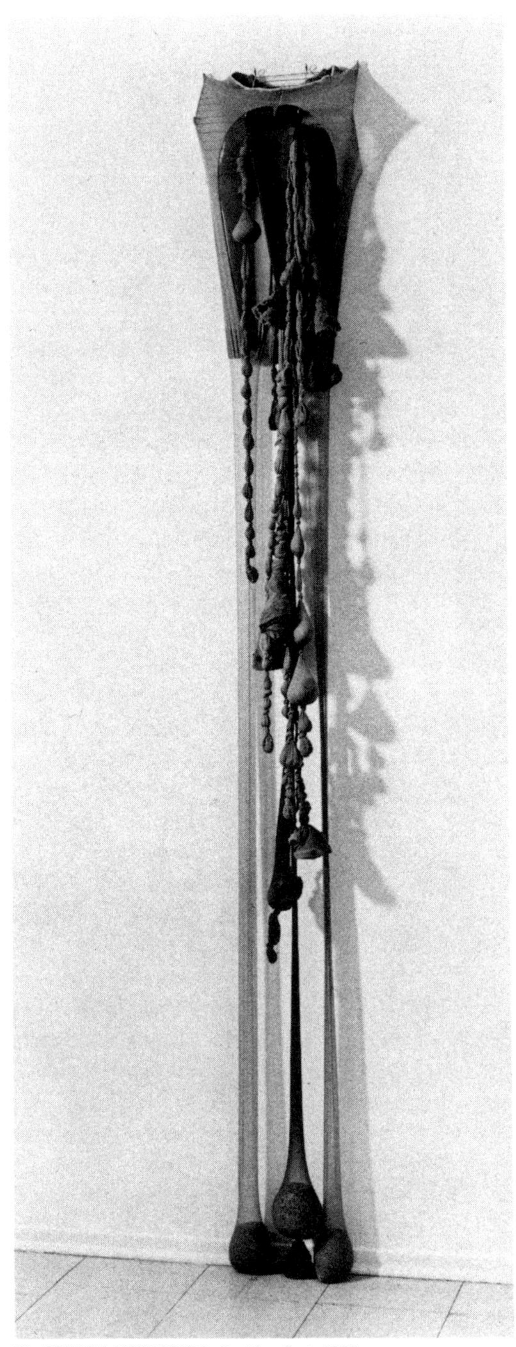

29. SENGA NENGUDI. *Insides Out. 1977*

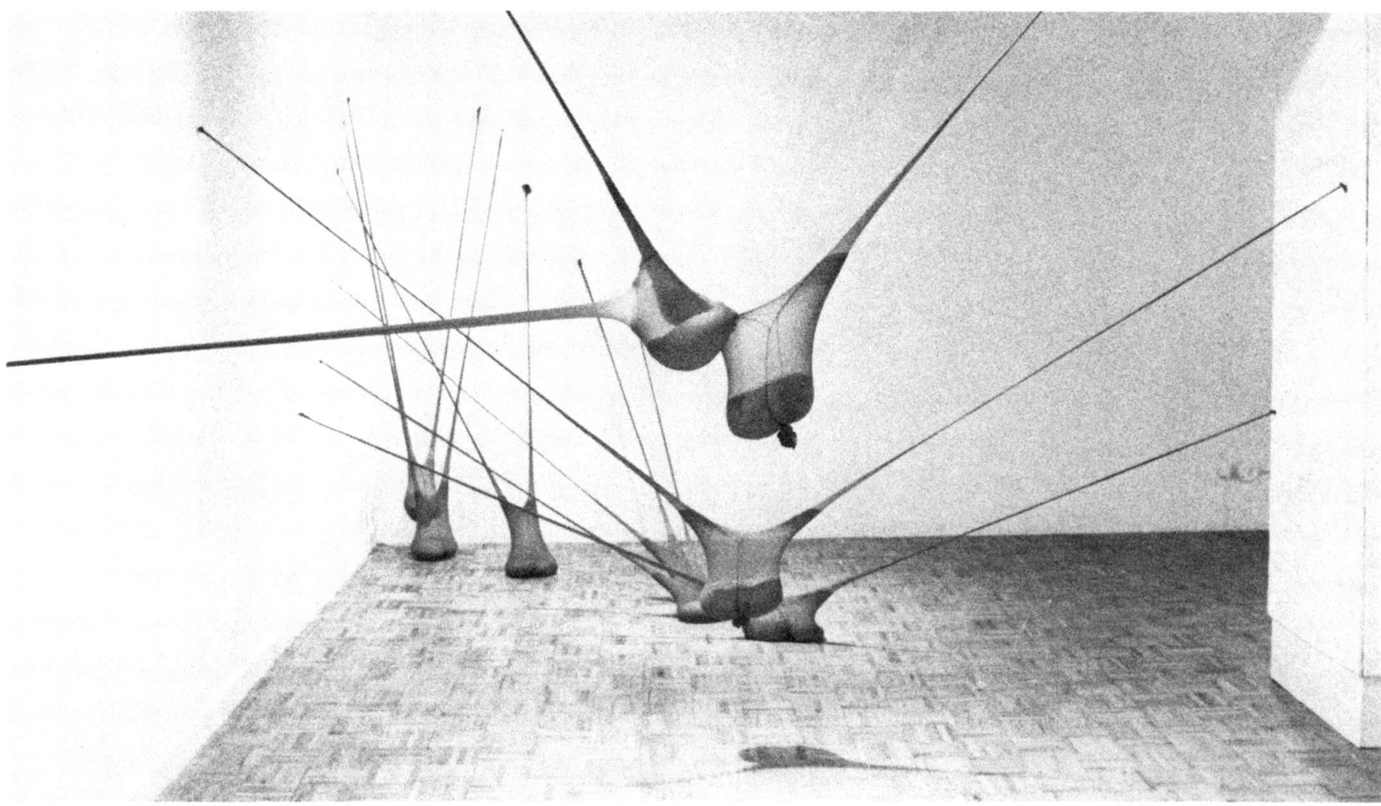

30. SENGA NENGUDI. *I. 1977*

ton restricts the space utilized. The wall and floor are not incorporated, as with Nengudi, into the structural composition of the works. While tension and release achieve a greater prominence and dominance in Nengudi's works due to the elasticity of the nylon mesh, Hamilton is able to condense and maintain a similar effect through larger and more isolated tied and knotted bags, and by increasing and emphasizing the amount and size of the threaded areas. The result is a more static, less fluid, structure in which tightly stuffed textural cloth provide the focal interest.

Discards and remains, which she constantly collects, constitute the material in Hamilton's works. *Love Letter, 1977* (fig. 37) combines paper, muslin, painted canvas, string and metal into a horizontal wall hanging of varying textural surfaces constituting four layers or levels. As in most of her wall hangings, the metal is placed on top of the material and is primarily used as contradictory accents to the malleable structure and shapes. Here the circular metal disc are placed below five corresponding drawn "X"es. Their smooth and rusted surface acts as a textural device reinforcing the woven canvas, the ground for the smooth textured and stuffed muslin. Emphasizing the horizontal pull, the muslin is stretched, tied and bound by string that is attached to the corners of tattered uneven parallel boundaries. The layering and juxtaposition of textures and stuffed and knotted muslin allude to a certain mysticism and secrecy, intriguing and disconcerting as the inner privacy of her world is concealed.

In *Option: Continuance, 1977* (fig. 38) Hamilton's juxtaposition of materials and structural placement becomes less intimate as visual interest is virtually restricted to balance and counter-balance, form and non-form.

Hamilton's recent works are reminiscent of totems. A vertical narrative of images is created by varying the types of cloth and materials which are wrapped around thin rods of steel and bound by plastic cord. In these works the cord

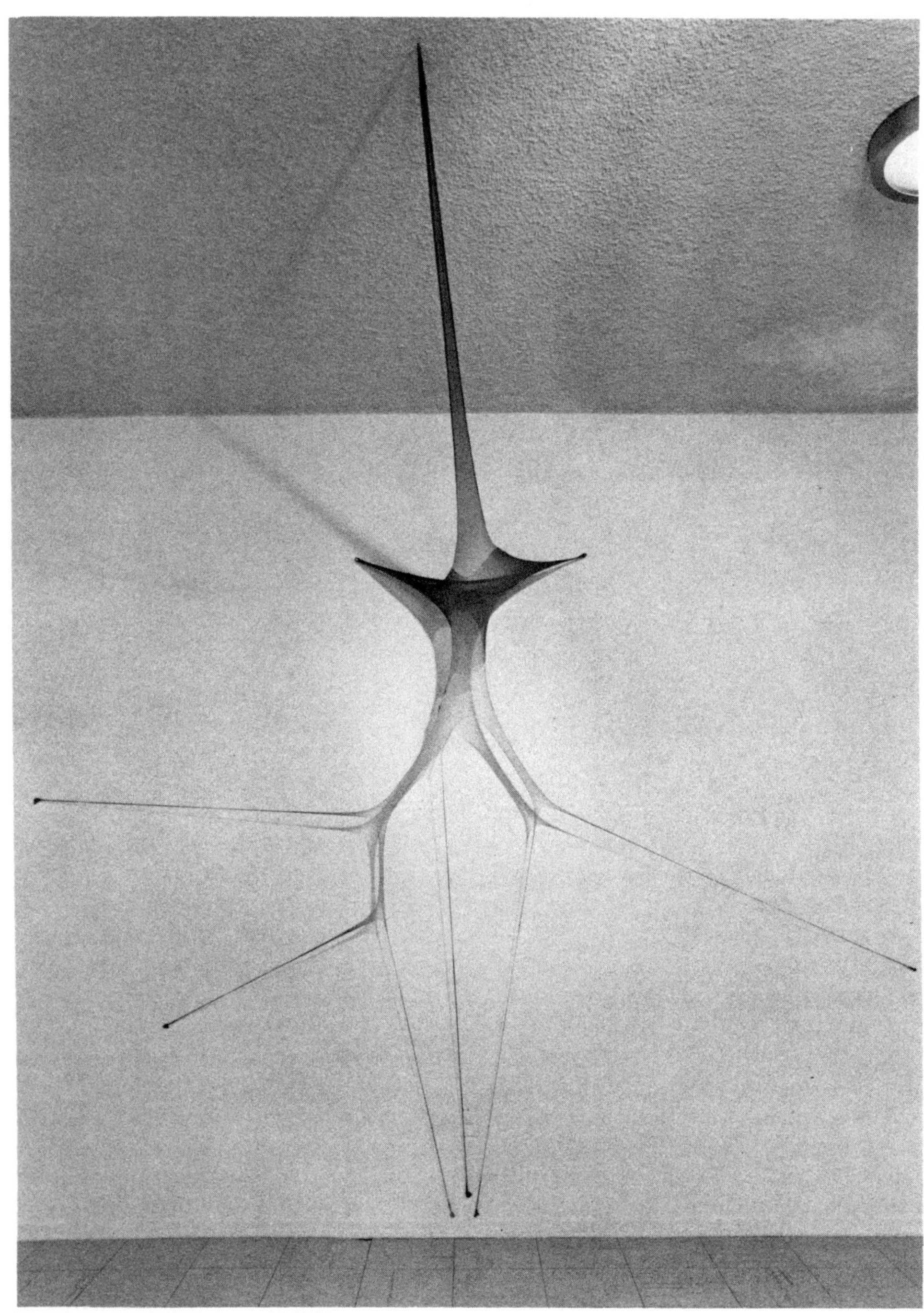

32. SENGA NENGUDI. *Internal I. 1977*

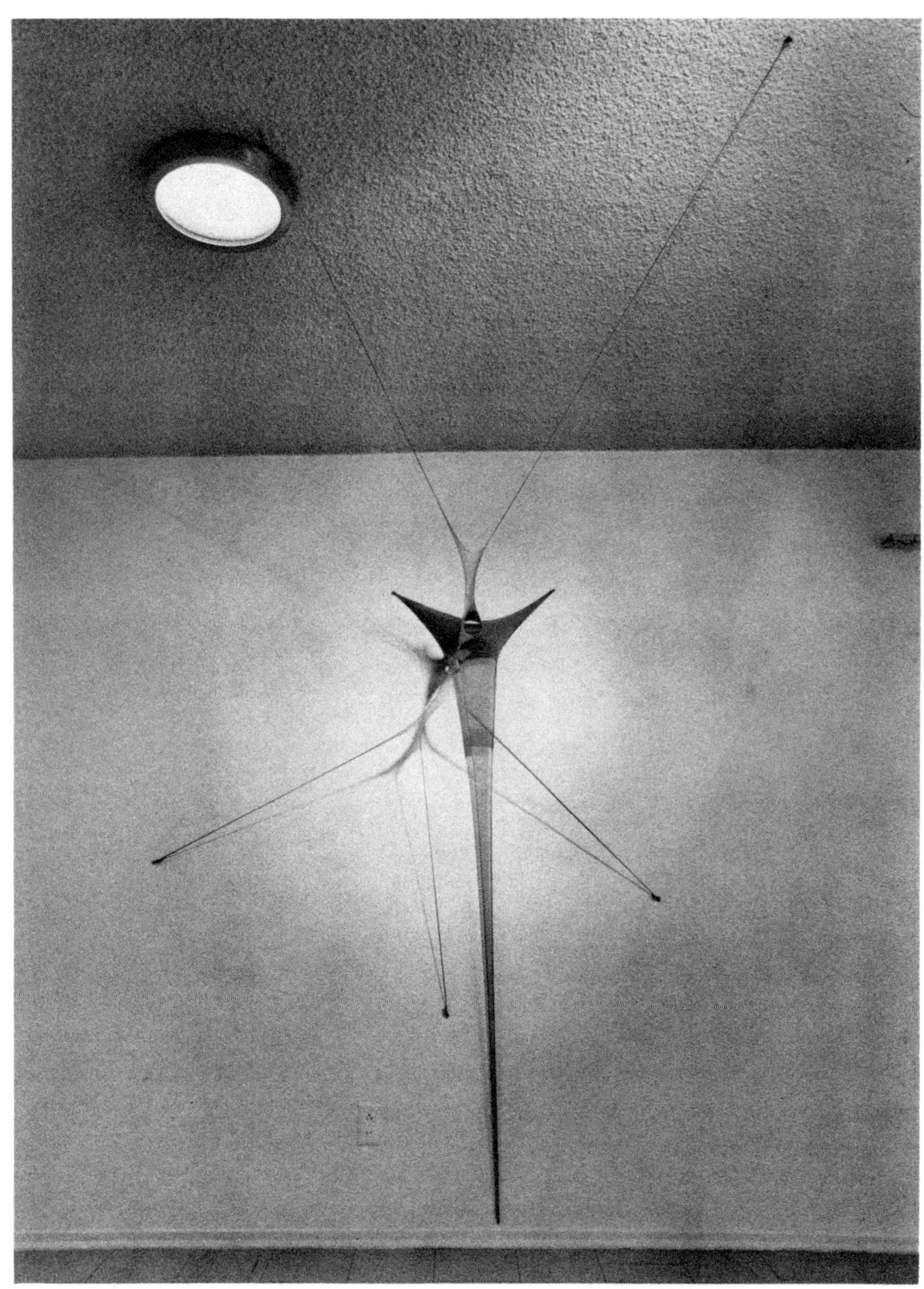

33. SENGA NENGUDI. *Internal II. 1977*

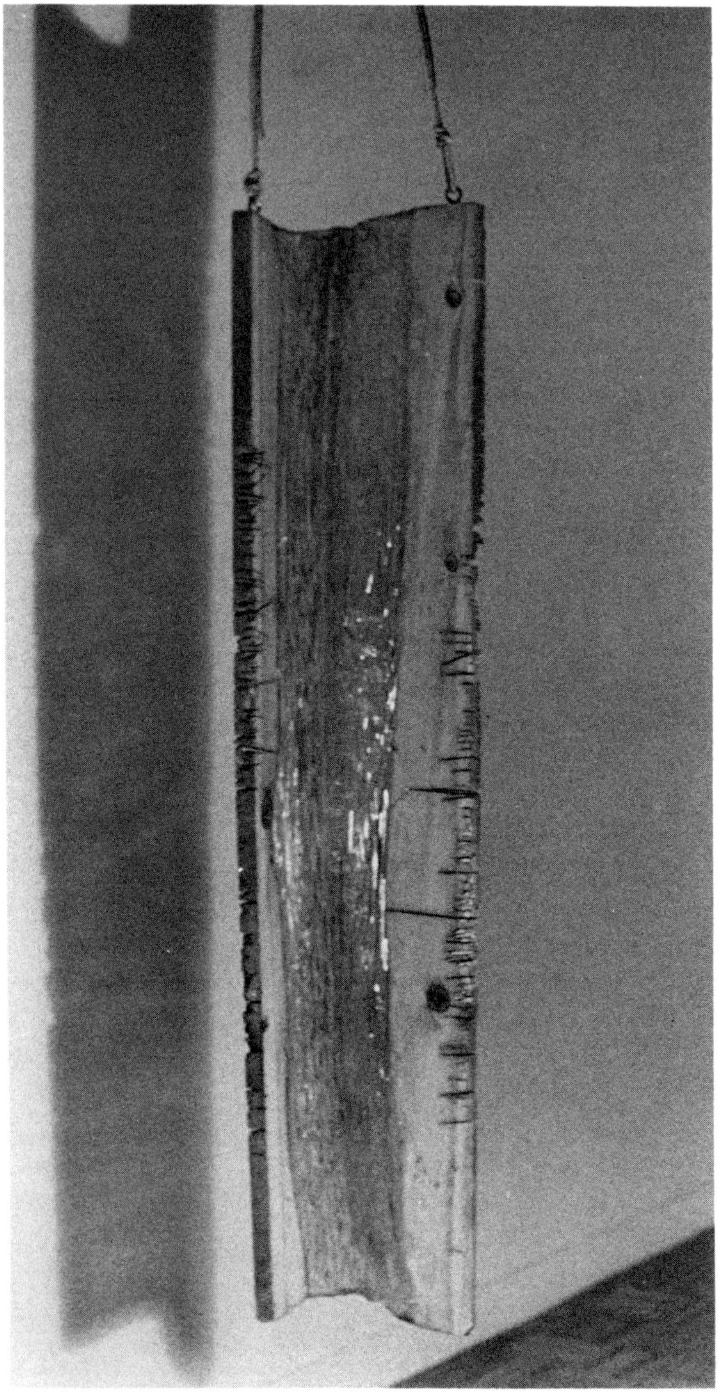

34. SUSAN FITZSIMMONS. *Water—Summer. 1977*

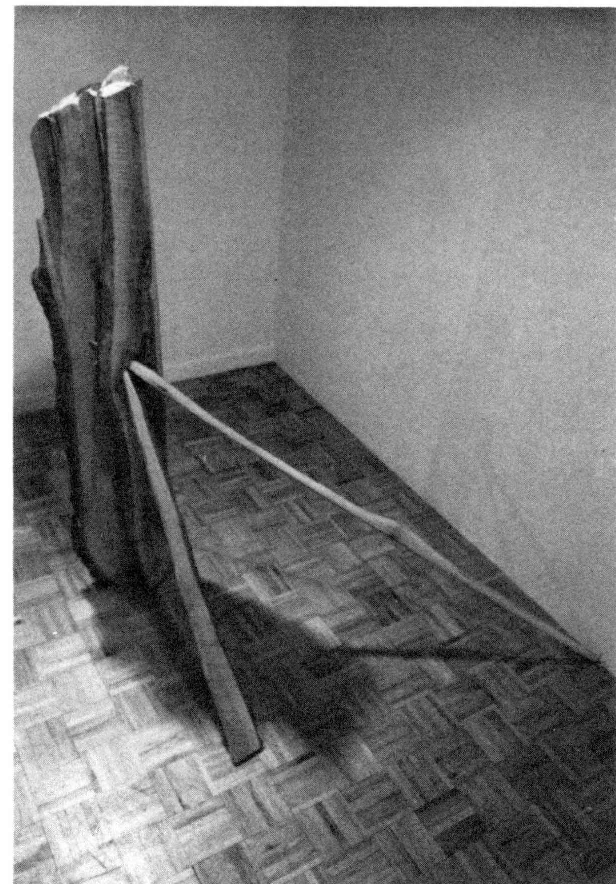

35. SUSAN FITZSIMMONS. *Water—Fall. 1977*

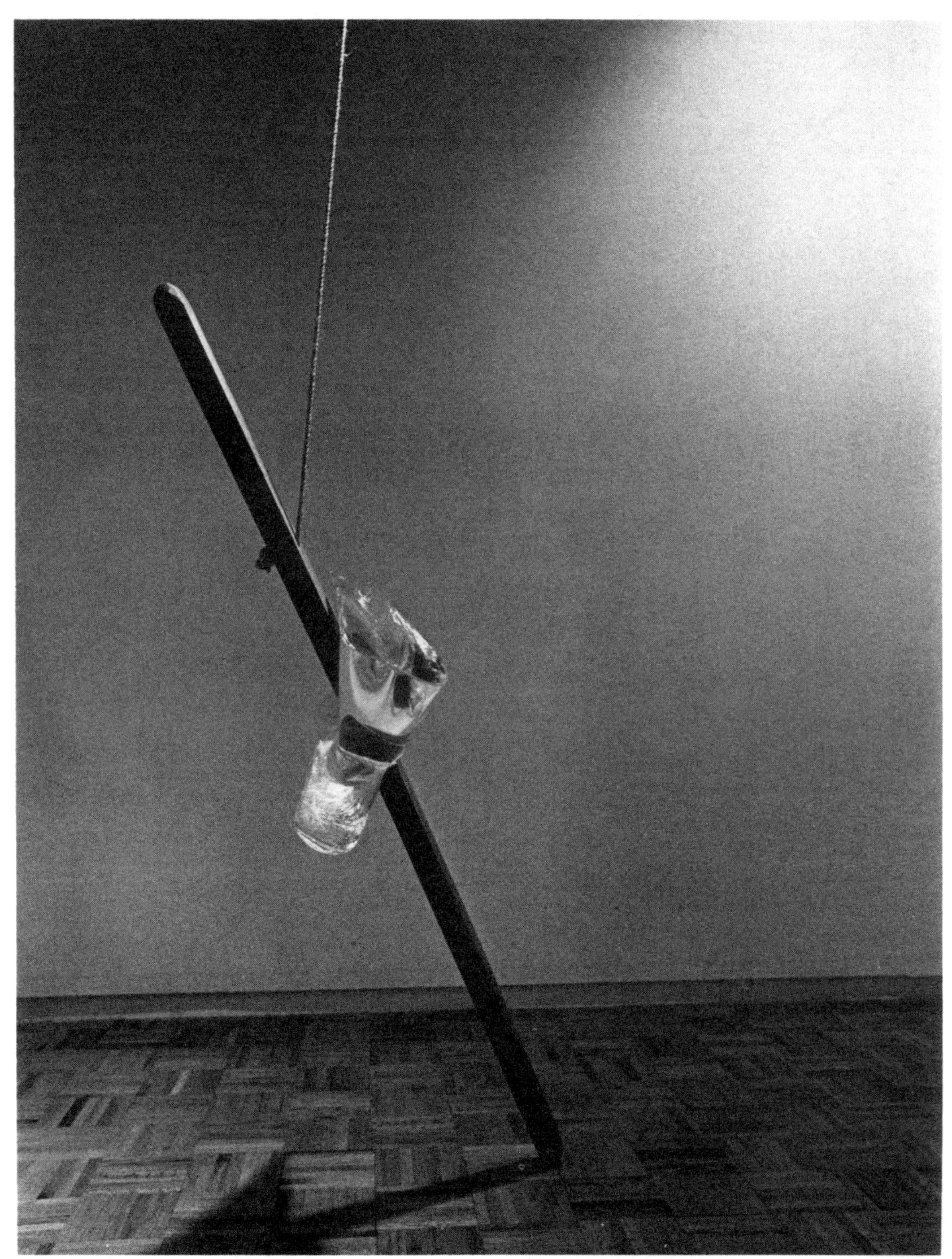

36. SUSAN FITZSIMMONS. *Stick-Caught Cube. 1977*

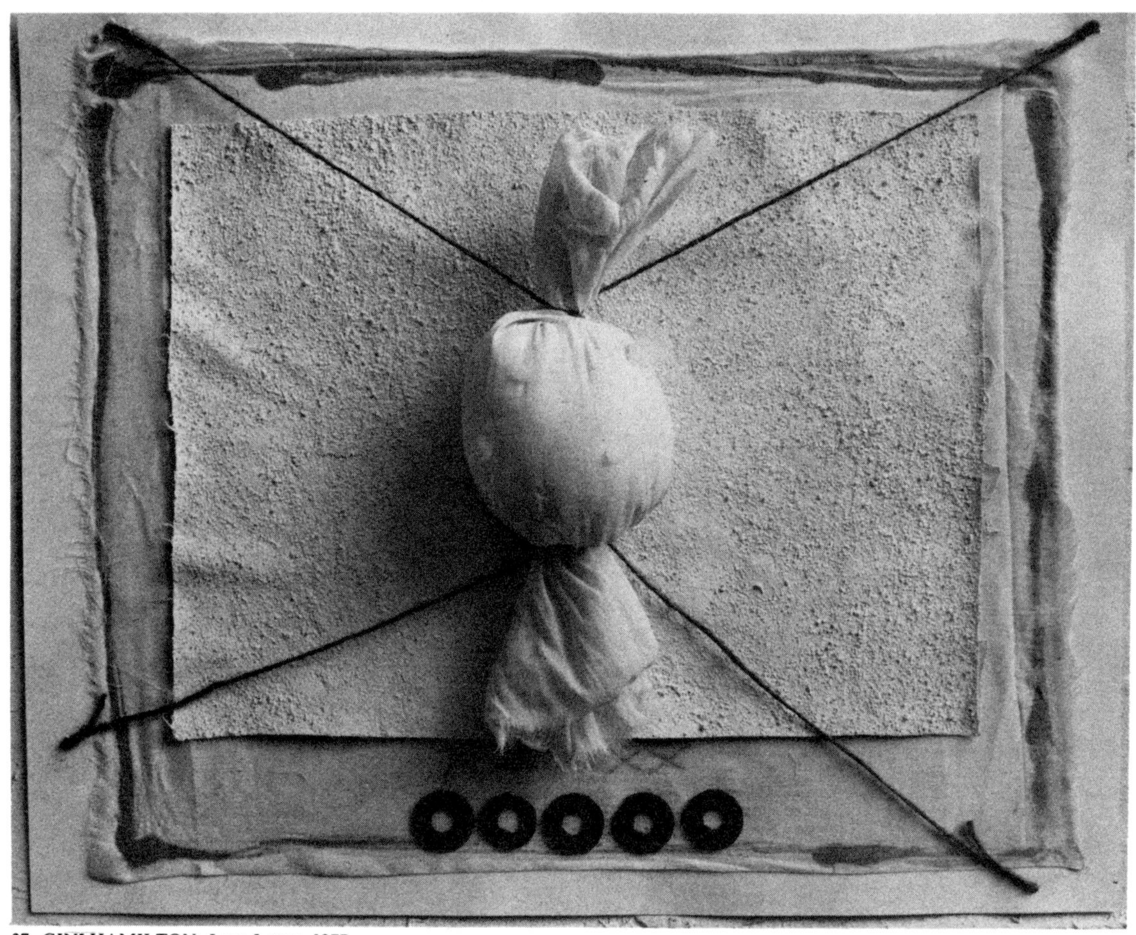

37. **GINI HAMILTON.** *Love Letter. 1977*

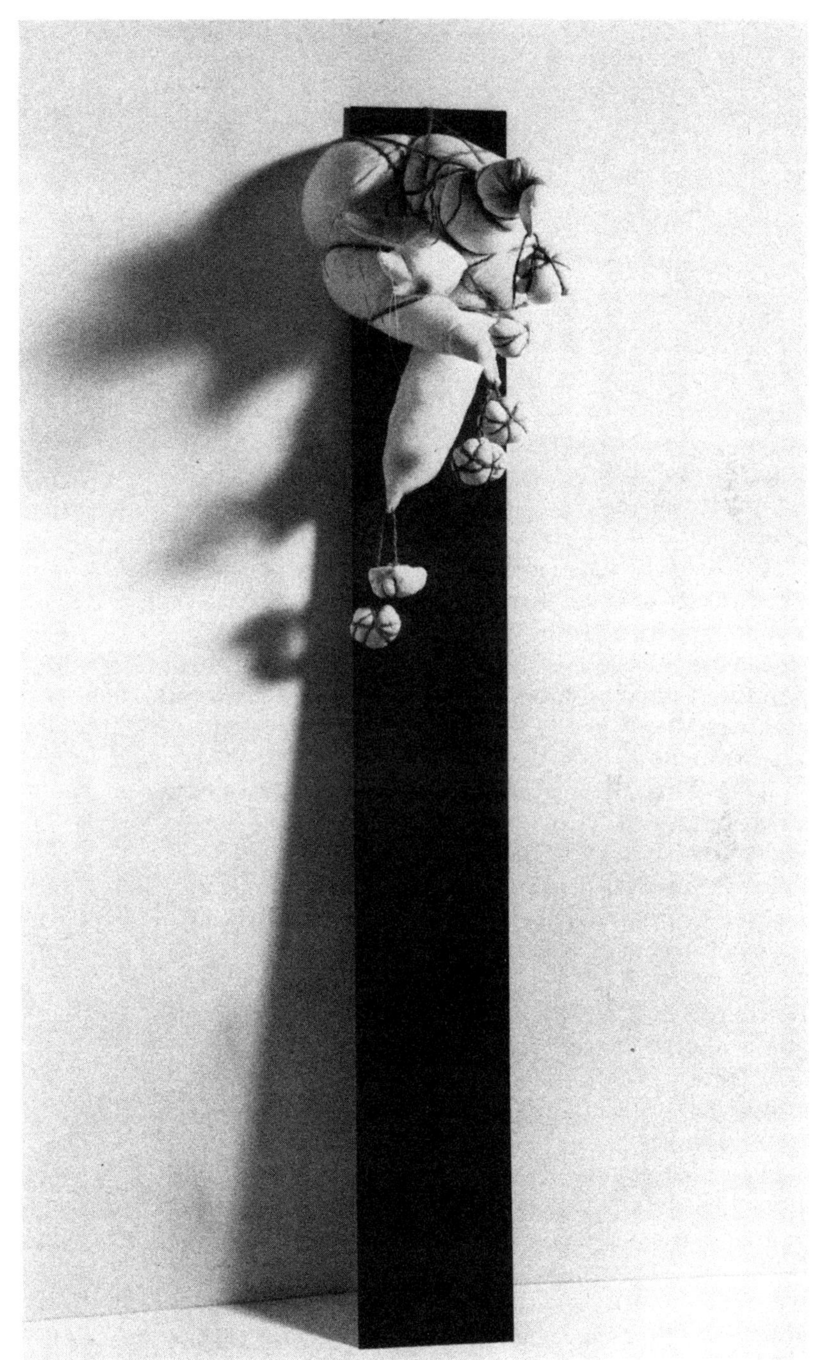

38. GINI HAMILTON. *Option: Continuance. 1977*

acts as the support for the steel as it wraps around the material and the rod separating the images into sections. The cord is then stretched and nailed onto the wall, positioning the rod in a diagonal slant. The works appear intimate, as the lace acts as the dominant textural element concealing and exposing bits and pieces of information to the viewer.

"My art comes out of me . . . my knowledge about myself is more complete . . . I have a link with my history . . . my feminism."[39]

A personal, almost solipsistic searching is contained within the contextural iconography of Wendy Ward Ehlers. Creating visual serials, Ehlers' works act as two- and three-dimensional diaries which contain her cumulative experiences, observations and interpretations of her external and inner self. Her primary materials are remains which she collects from her day-to-day activities and from nature.

Awakened by the need to "own something"[40], in 1972 Ehlers began to collect various types of discards from rags and bones to rusty nails. Ownership declared, she concerned herself with identifying them and making them important. A series of works emerged made from her collected items. They were encased, labeled and designated as belonging to the "Ehlers Collection." Immediately she began to concern herself with ownership of space. Environments developed which acted as markings or areas of space which she possessed. In 1974, Ehlers began to use clothes dryer lint as the primary material in her works. Encased in plexiglass boxes, these clumped and enmeshed bodies of untransformed material act as autobiographical portraits and narratives which are, at times, documented through notations signifying the day, week and month in which each row or square was collected from the wash.

In *Traces, 1974/75* (pl. 10) Ehlers pushes the lint through slats of wood. With the natural grain of the wood, exposed and patined, the texture and color nuances of the lint provide a gestural and tactile surface. The wood slats act as a barred restraint in which the lint struggles and pulls through for breath and exposure.

The lint is fully exposed in *Three Inches Equals One Week of Laundry, 1974* (fig. 39), twenty-one plexi-boxed squares of lint. Textural and color subtleties make up the surface field as the lint is pushed and squeezed within the confines of the plexi container. The intent was to provide documentation of the artist's history as her concept of scale was based on cumulative small images placed in a subliminal grid, and rendered collectively as a single unit.

In 1974, Ehlers began to place cereal on the lint surface. Individual pieces of cereal from "Lucky Charms" to "Alphabits" were ordered by a grid system in the foreground of the picture plane. The color of the cereal acted as an accent to the color-hazed background, affecting textural divisions and interplays.

As a result of her observation of people viewing art in museums and galleries, Ehlers became interested in placing the art work in unexpected areas. From these observations she concluded that people immediately go to the labels rather than the art object itself. In an attempt to seemingly disturb this ritual, she created a 150 foot floor piece of lint contained in wood crates rendering it like the lint one finds around a baseboard.

In 1975, Ehlers began her series of feather works. Primarily using pheasant feathers she placed them behind wood slats or allowed them to stand free on wooden bases. *Feather Floor Piece, 1977* (fig. 40) shows an apparent allegiance to the natural design and movement contained within the feathers since she built an almost pyramidal form which projects from a wooden base. The tactile quality of her works continues, as the color and the slick and fuzzy texture of the feathers entice the senses.

During this time a series of works with twigs emerged. Bound together and free standing or placed on the wall as individual and interrelating notations, they seem to lyrically define space in isolation and or in collective groups. At times they appear as hieroglyphs; at other times they appear to be fetishes or unidentifiable utilitarian objects. Maintaining the order of the lint works, these twigs are placed in an almost sequenced pattern, often to be read vertically as if a tabloid or scroll.

An irony is suggested in Ehlers' works. An almost satirical suggestion is combined with apparent internal and mental searching for clarified and ultimately proclaimed definitions of her relative position to external and internal contexts. Her process is intuitive, a feeling and sense rather than a formulated or intellectual method or idea. Her works are about "myths of myths,"[41] her own culture, her own narrative. She uses remains and natural material since they possess another life prior to their incorporation into her works. Ehlers forms and constructs her works from the physical, perceptual and metaphysical properties of these materials as well as from the elements which constitute her own reality and life cycle.

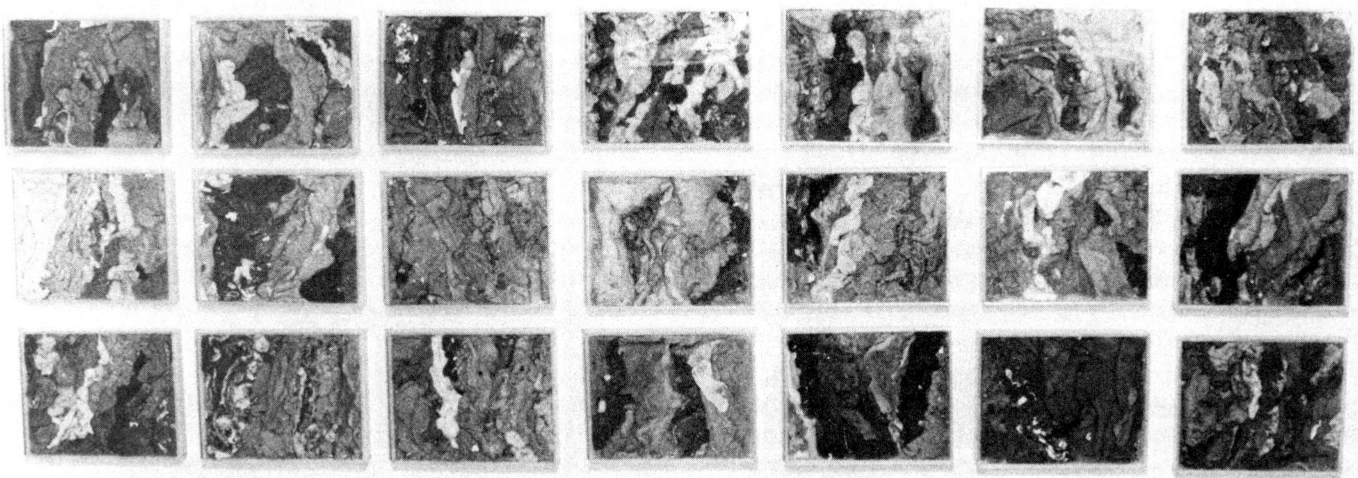

39. WENDY EHLERS. *Three Inches Equals One Week Of Laundry. 1974*

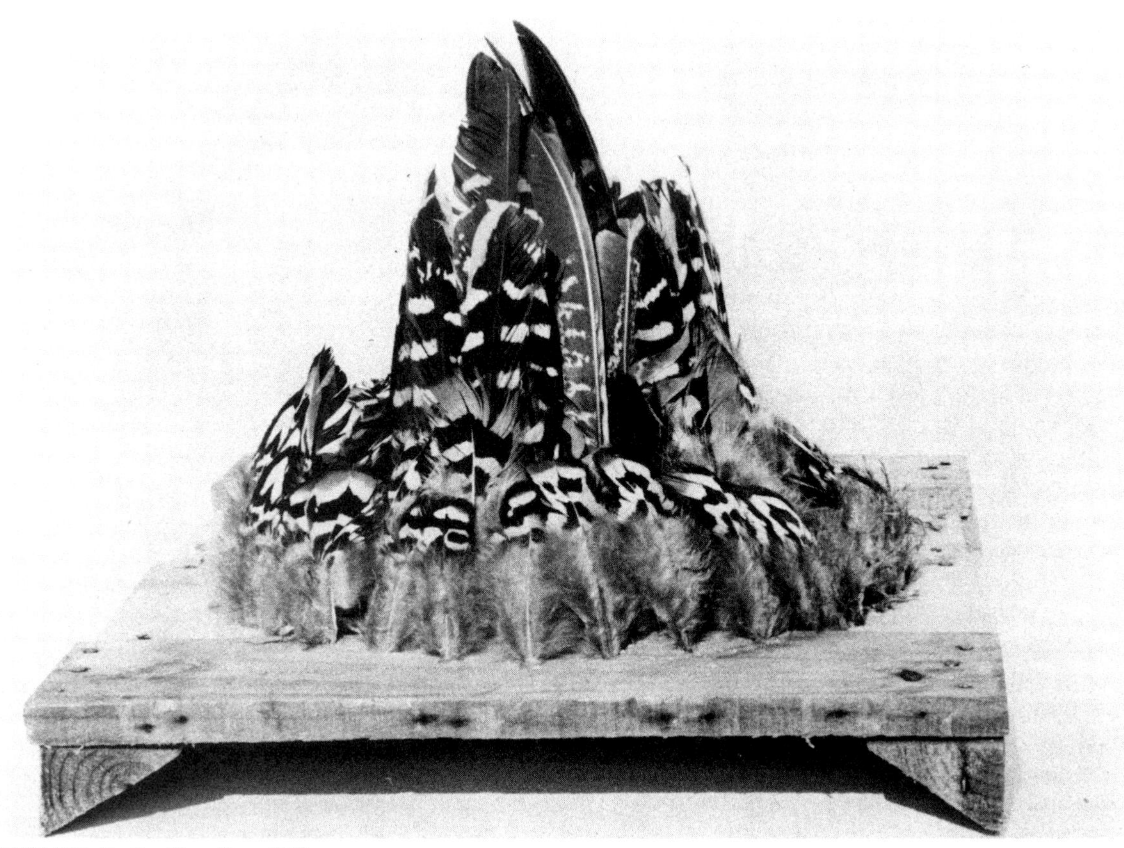

40. WENDY EHLERS. *Feather Floor Piece. 1977*

Betye Saar's work is intuitive, mystical, personal, intimate, ritualistic, referential, private and collective. Made from remains and found items, they too possessed another life, belonged to someone else and contained a past and a present history which she formulated into an accumulative consciousness and memory through context.

Prior to 1969, Saar worked in design and graphics. Her early prints incorporated symbols of the occult from astrology to phrenology. It was in 1969-1970 that she found an old " leaded" window onto which she glued her prints and framed them. This method catalyzed her interest in three-dimensional concepts resulting in a series of window works. Termed "Hoodo" she continued to incorporate the symbols of the occult providing a mystical background to the windows. The use of windows symbolically provides the viewer the ability to perceive on varying levels of consciousness.

The next series of works she termed "Mojo." Primarily wall hangings, they consist of mystical symbols incorporated with natural objects ranging from pods and driftwood to feathers, shells, bones and leather. These hangings act as protective charms, with Saar drawing contemporary parellels between her art and the mystical artifacts of non-western societies.

Saar is concerned with the metaphysical, referential and spiritual qualities embodied within the natural, organic and man-made objects she recycles. Primarily, she focuses on objects which are purely for display and those which have an essential power. Working intuitively, she collects these items over a period of time. As she puts them together the theme for each work evolves. A search for a title is intrinsically involved in her process as it literally translates the ritualistic meaning of the works to the viewer. Ritual is a major component in her process in which she becomes the transit from which the art object evolves. " . . . the medium and energy or the force which is the cumulative consciousness goes through me and produces all the work I leave behind."[42]

After sifting through and selecting the objects which will be used in a composition, she puts them all in and then begins to extract them in order to clarify space and balance. Her spaces are intentional providing psychological intrusions in which the viewer is invited to participate in finding the underlying meanings of the work. The viewer's participation is as personal and intimate as the objects themselves since images and artifacts provide a referential guide as well as a departure point in which the viewer can insert his/her own personal experiences and observations, memories and consciousness. The works act as universal and personal data allowing for general and specific interpretations and responses.

Saar is concerned with inducing all five of the senses as she incorporates touch, smell, taste, sound and visual elements within the works. Suggestions of natural elements are apparent as images signifying air, fire, water and earth are intertwined throughout the compositions.

By 1973, influenced by socio-political activities, her works became political and nostalgic. Utilizing black imagery, the objects become "symbols of the past to communicate the realities of the present and the uncertainties of the future."[43] The Aunt Jemima series evolved. Utilizing this stereotypical image, Saar places Aunt Jemima in context with the essence and intricate external and internal psyche and conditions in which the image exists. "In the beginning General Mills selected a black woman to play Aunt Jemima and she went around saying, 'I's in town, honey.' But she is also representative of all the black women who worked as mammies or house servants. They covered their hair that way and wore that kind of apron. She was a woman who could cook, who was full of love, a family person. The characterization was negative in that the black woman could only be seen as an Aunt Jemima or else she was seen as a hooker, a piece of property . . . to be used whenever (he) felt like it . . . I take the figure that classifies all black women and make her into one of the leaders of the revolution—although she is a pretty strong character anyway."[44]

As a result of her images of pickaninnies, Black Sambos and Aunt Jemima, Saar became interested in history and tradition. Folk altars resulted which display the contextural progression of human existence. In *Last Dance, 1975* (fig. 41) figural imagery is replaced by intimate and private souvenirs and artifacts. This multi-object textural work sorts and assembles relics from time and experience. The viewer is seduced into a psychological world of beings and spirits provoking a curiosity for understanding and restructuring the individuals privately exposed within the box. This immediate curiosity is turned into personal remembrances, times, places, love, dance, the individual and intimate wanderings of the viewer's mind, releasing hidden or misplaced time and experiences.

Saar's recent works are larger in scale creating structures

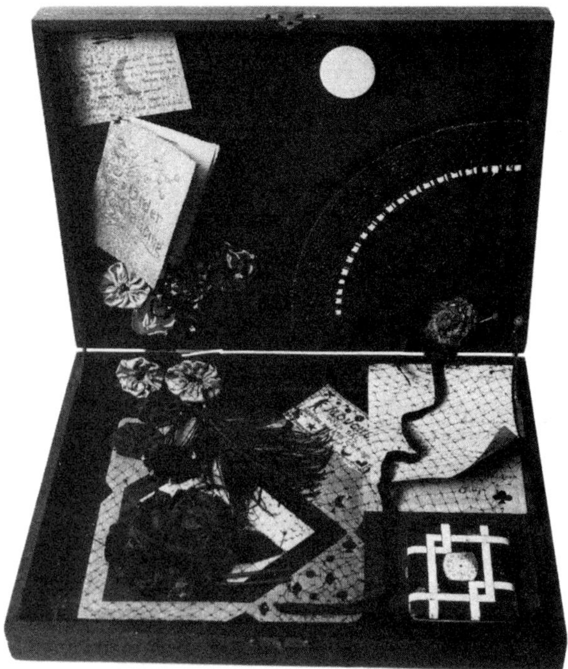

41. BETYE SAAR. *Last Dance. 1975*

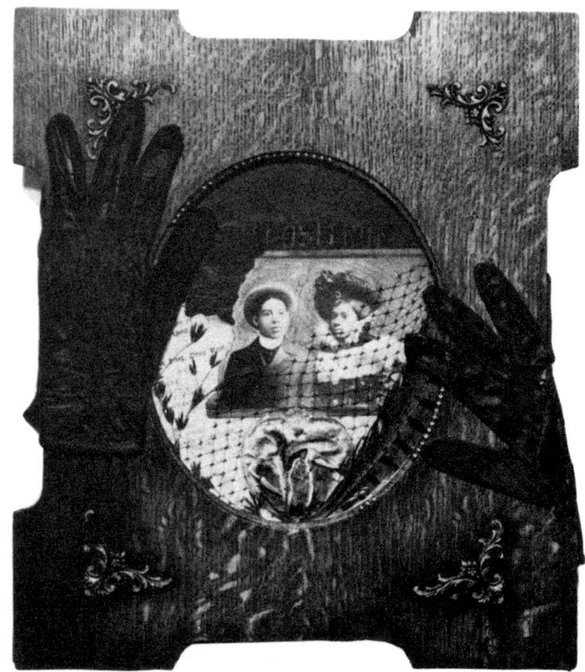

42. BETYE SAAR. *Ohne Hast, Ohne Rast. 1976*

resembling shrines or thrones in which the physical and spiritual realms interact. Fetish-stools *(Indigo Mercy, 1975)* or totems, *(Spirit Catcher, 1976-77)* combine the materials of display and power into private and collective pasts.[45]

The private is accentuated in the torn and tattered photograph of *Ohne Hast, Ohne Rast, 1976* (fig. 42). Contained within a wooden frame, it portrays people known and unknown in a psychological displacement with objects and symbols of past and present times. The gloves deceive the viewer since they infer that someone is looking in from the outside or from behind as the photograph becomes a face of encased memories.

Rites and rituals, the past and present, the private yet universal form the content of Betye Saar's works providing context meanings to the disassembled often discarded or neglected essence of human existence.

Rites and rituals embody the essence of Houston Conwill's works. In a more literal translation of African concepts into contemporary experiences than occurs in the works of Hammons or Saar, Conwill creates two-dimensional works which act as foils for ritual performances that involve the artist as griot (storyteller) and the viewer as initiated members of his rites.

Casting and pulling roplex and latex from molds, he sews these forms together as "leaves in a book with all its pages exposed simultaneously."[46] He terms these forms petrigraphs because they resemble "petrified animal skins."[47] These leathery-skinned plaques are then embossed with patterns, insect forms, symbols and lines which act as heiroglyphic narratives of stories, tales and myths referring to past and present human experiences. Unlike Fitzsimmons, who exposes and integrates the states of natural and technological phenomena, Conwill alludes to organic material through an illusionistic surface produced by a variety of paint application and technique in order to produce earth-like hues and textures which suggest organic exposure to natural elements.

Initially Conwill worked in a Gilliam-like paint-wash and canvas folding technique. Since 1974, however, his works have evolved into spiritual and ritualistic commentaries on modern conditions. His theory and method are based on energy and power sources which result from age and continued use. He terms his works Juju a "generic name for African magic and power practices"[48] since his beliefs are based on energy rather than matter as the true nature of things. The nature of things can be controlled by man, as the energy can be controlled through ritual.[49] The reuse and age of the object determine the level of power that it will contain.

These petrigraphs act as memory aids during the ritual. Each contains informational systems of primal icons resulting in a story or tale; a map of human activity and environmental textures.[50]

Recurrent images on the petrigraphs are the roach, fish and alligator. A gut bucket (symbolizing the food remains given slaves and the base level of emotion or experience), a goblet and a ceremonial stool are three-dimensional objects in which the petrigraphs' narratives and ritual performance are incorporated (pl. 11).

Conwill gives meanings to his imagery as the roach signifies plague or bad times; the fish, the sign of life; and the alligator, the messenger. The ritual acts as a cleansing process in which the artist is joined by ancestors to celebrate survival and life.[51] The texture of the work reminds one of body scarifications. In *Edison Tale* (fig. 43) the surface of the petrigraph takes on landscape qualities as identifiable objects and personal notations provide the content narrative of the work.

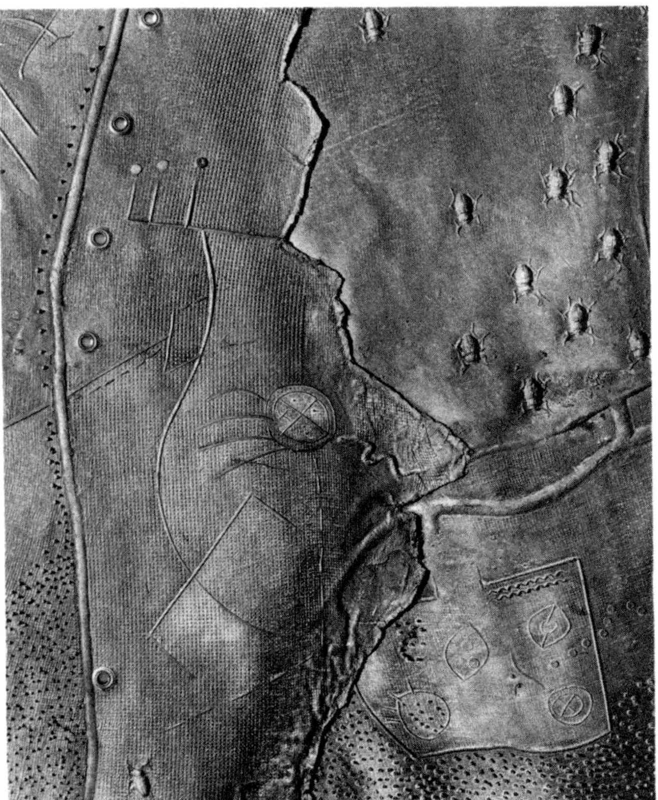

43. HOUSTON CONWILL. *Edison Tale (Detail). 1976*

Music is a prominent element in these ritual-works. Initially using spirituals and the blues, Conwill incorporates music in order to "bombard the ears with sounds . . ."[52] thus activating additional sensory participation. He often uses saw dust to induce the sense of smell.

Since 1976 Conwill has incorporated a metallic quality with a more vivid palette. In addition he has included traditional African music in his rituals which increases the emotional purging of the participants and provides an even more direct and literal connection with African traditions.

While Conwill's art theoretically concerns the conjuring of energy, powers and spirits through contemporary iconography and ritual, it perceptually considers the distinct and similar properties inherent to both modern and ancient technology and primal existence. Contexturally, Conwill provides definition and redefinition, leading the viewer into the surrealistic notations of human thought through maps, formulas and images of the real and spiritual realms of human existence.

Secrets, magic, mysticism, intimacies and myths intricately compose the iconography of Donna Byars. Primarily utilizing organic remains and natural phenomena as the material and substance of her art, Byars creates two- and three-dimensional floor and wall works which expose, contain and conceal the emotive and psychological interplays of fetish-like apparitions.

Referred to as " . . . an archeologist of our own culture, studying its waste, rather than an anthropologist of others, miming their rituals,"[53] Byars works intuitively, collecting, sorting and assembling these urban findings into abstract vignettes which seemingly depict the metaphysical history and present conditions of modern society.

Her apparitions are evasive, whether placed in boxes, behind bars, stretched on walls or free-standing. They appear to tease from behind their frontal structure. A movement flees to a corner; a shadow or a whisper peeks from a crevice or superimposes itself between the folds and textures of the material. Although her imagery is often contained, it defies static conditions, vibrating and shimmering as if possessed by spirits which choose to speak, or remain silent as they taunt the viewer with ephemeral reflections of the results of past and present existence.

Many of her image-objects display a history of neglect. The isolation and happenstance of their conditions are afforded a platform in her contextural application. The viewer is provoked to participate in these recollections as he/she remembers the time, place and experience shared and associated with these images' messages.

The textural and decayed qualities of the objects' surfaces account for their tactile seduction. Splintered, worn wood, hair, skeletons and feathers are some of the organic substances which suggest the previous physical life of these works. While small and contained they dominate the environment with their spiritual and dramatic overtones that seemingly penetrate the atmosphere.

The content of these works is often predicated on subconscious stimuli. *Oracle Stone's Grove, 1977* (fig. 44) developed from a dream about an old woman who, speaking in vapors, spewed forth eternal truths. During these confessions the woman began to slip from her chair. Rescued from slipping into the ground, the woman turned to stone, no longer able to speak.[54] After this dream, Byars accidentally came upon two large stones found near a construction sight. Having just read an article on the Delphic Oracle and having attended a lecture on mythology, Byars incorporated all of these elements, both cryptic and self-existant, resulting in this three-dimensional setting. The stone laden rocking chair sits as an altar among the live foliage of trees. The stones, although partially destroyed, retain their maximum force and appear to have an inner life as they sit proudly atop the rocking chair. Wind and/or other natural forces allow the rocker to move back and forth without human interference or initiation thus providing the element of unexpected movement which adds to the feelings of spiritual lurkings within.

Aged and worn effects are prominent in *Rabbit Pen—A Reclamation, 1976* (fig. 45). A cage acts as a jail cell for a tiny, defenseless rabbit whose spirit seems to prevade the construction. Not only a captive of the box, the rabbit is swathed in bandages. Two clay pots hang precariously over the rabbit's head heightening the eerie and vague feeling of discomfort. Despite these encumbrances, the tiny eyes of the rabbit peer dolefully toward the viewer as if some kind of inner life has taken over his inanimate body.

The perceptual effects of caging or enclosure tend to induce the viewer inward rather than repelling or rejecting

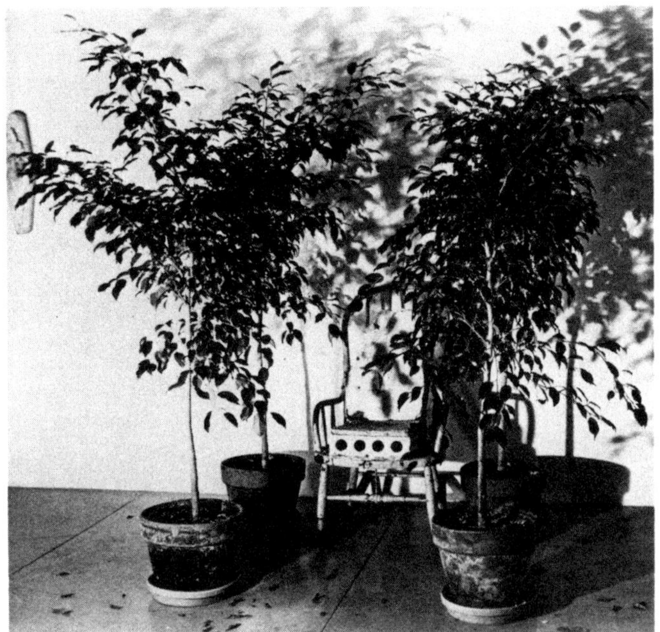

44. DONNA BYARS. *Oracle Stone's Grove. 1977*

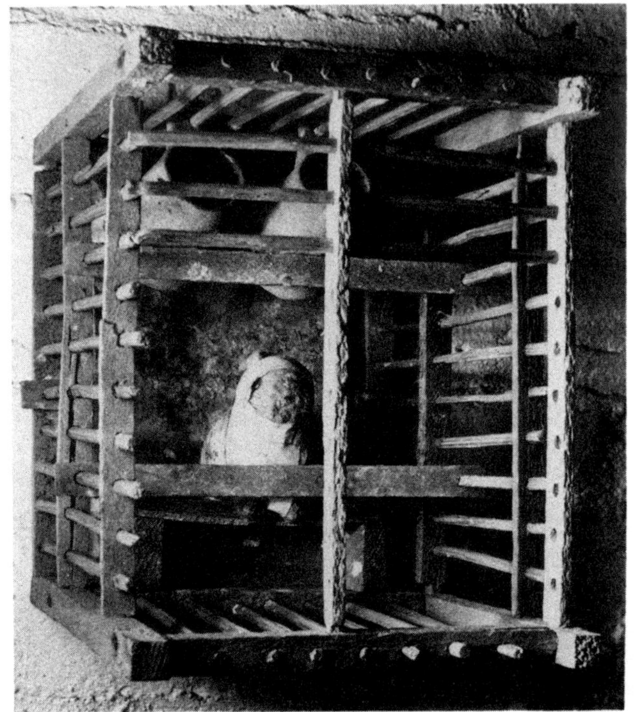

45. DONNA BYARS. *Rabbit Pen—A Reclamation. 1976*

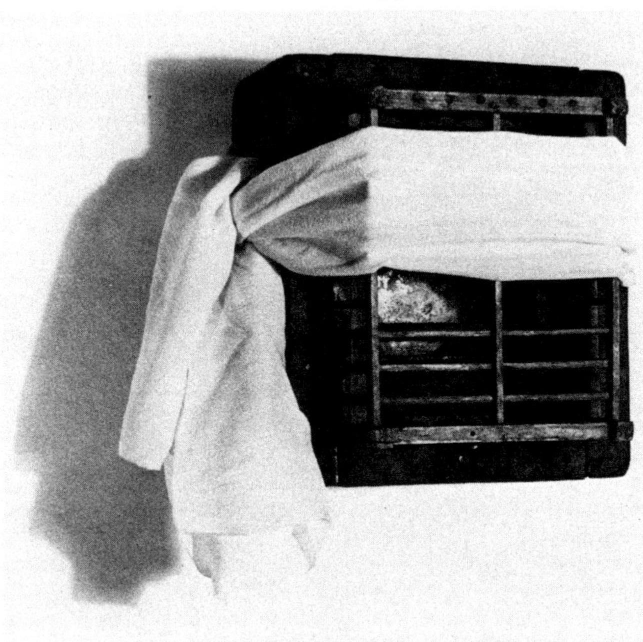

46. DONNA BYARS. *Vested Relic. 1977*

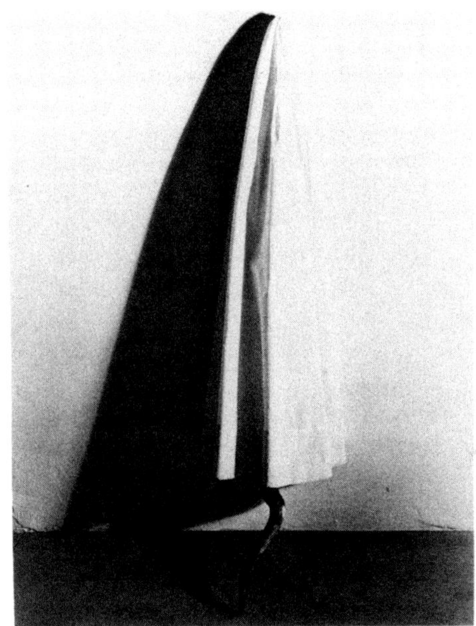

47. DONNA BYARS. *The Secret.* 1977

participation. These enclosures are constructed in such a manner that curiosity forces the viewer to inspect or peer into the hidden action or mysteries. By binding the cage in *Vested Relic, 1977* (fig. 46) the objects contained within become more intriguing as the prevailing shadows only highlight certain portions of the enclosed objects creating drama from within.

Byars reduces the number of objects which comprise *The Secret, 1977* (fig. 47) providing the viewer with a limited iconography to interpret. This piece, as the title implies, appears to react against the revelation of the inner self. *The Secret* is graceful and sinuously delicate. The cloth, an antique muslin petticoat draped over a carved stick, does not succeed in inhibiting the suggestion of activity and energy which appear to be occuring underneath. One's interest and curiosity is heightened by the enclosure created by this fabric as the viewer is almost dared to peek underneath, or to pull the cloth away altogether. The viewer is left to surmise, therefore, what the petticoat covers. The use of a woman's undergarment and the phallic suggestion of the curved support hint at something sexual and provocative.

The past becomes present in Byars' context as the viewer is forced from passivity, dared to forget and challenged to remember.

Numbers and arrows provide the referential linkage between order and disorder, and content and thematic elements in the personal iconography of Howardena Pindell.

Sharing the other Contexturalists concern for energy, mysticism, automatism and ritualistic process, Pindell, after the mid 1960s, moved from figurative renderings influenced by de Kooning. Interested in points (dots or spots) as substance, Pindell began to work with ellipses in dot patterning exploring field and illusionary space by 1968. Reminiscent of Poons, Pindell's canvases were influenced by the imagery of microscopic chemical systems and bonds. Like an amoeba in water, her biomorphic forms float in space on the canvases' surface. Uniformly placed dots and brush strokes on the canvas provided the atmospheric conditions of her optical fields, comprised of color and form.

Pindell began her collection and use of remains in works dating from 1969. Initially she selected the one-quarter inch point in the making of her templates. These templates consisted of the one-quarter inch dot uniformly achieved by punching holes into paper. After, color was sprayed through the holes forming the dot imagery. The one-quarter inch punchings were saved and used in works dating from 1973. The dot imagery of her early 1970s canvases covered the entire surface providing a variety of visual effects resulting from movement, light and form. Her use of a grid or underlying system is apparent yet contradicted by de-emphasizing the geometric, rendering the grid in an almost imperceivable state and accentuating the lack of order and the appearance of automatism through irregular shaped, unstretched canvases.

By 1973 a nonchromatic palette was used in the drawings made from the template remains, thereby making color incidental to the perceptual effects which occurred through form, structure and composition. Numbering the dots sequentially she initially used a grid-like ground as the structural format for the works. The numbered dots are placed in rows, adhering to the grid formation. This sequence, however, is ignored as they are placed numerically at random. *Untitled #4, 1973* (fig. 48) adheres to this format as the dots provide distinct yet similar contrasting characteristics.

Pindell's use of numbers evolved from her interest in ancient and modern writing. She felt number notations provided drawing-like qualities as well as a symbolism of modern language and culture. The numbers were employed to distinguish the dots as well as provide a reference for distance, size, mass, quantity and identification.

The second phase of her dot-numbered works also occurred in 1973. Scattering the dots across a surface of graph paper or three-dimensional grids she constructed from thread placed on top of a foundation board, she increased the random appearance of the dots accentuating the contrast between order and disorder. Using a spray adhesive, the dots connect in space forming three-dimensional structures. They hang, fall and intersect creating depth and a spatial vastness which occupies the total surface of the picture plane. The order and disorder of these works at times become synonymous. Essentially, while the individual numerical displacement and random positioning of the dots can be perceived as disorder, the overall effects provide a unified structure reenforced by identical dot size, and by the grid and surface density which creates a solid, undivided ordered effect. In these works Pindell incorporates powdered-like substances which enhance their tactile quality.

Pindell considers this process of order and disorder one of rearrangement, taking facts and information and rearranging the sequence in which they will be perceived. In her Letter Series this rearrangement and removal process are clearly apparent. Taking old letters, she cut, rearranged and combined their parts altering their original intent and individual context, as well as making the personal impersonal by their random and visible display.

By 1974, Pindell returned to the color palette. Removing the numbers from the dots, color now acts as the distinguishing characteristic. She maintained her overall use of space with no fixed focal point. Density and movement were increased through the opaque surface. Contradictions were continued as the overall effect of the work immediately implied static as well as active interweavings. The forms seem to float, yet are sustained. They appear heavy and weightless, continuous yet disjointed.

In 1975 Pindell began her use of arrows in her nonchromatic drawings to aid in distinguishing and determining speed, distance, action and position. She began to make her own paper in order to achieve a translucency in quality which was not possible in the 100% rag paper she previously had used. Translucent in nature, her paper provided spatial expansion as the numbered dots and arrows float in space through the front, middle and back layers of the paper.

During this period she altered her color drawing process. Essentially the drawings have been produced through her removal and rearranging method. She began first with a series of two-dimensional drawings made with acrylics, gouache, water-color and oil pastels. These drawings were then folded and punched. The resulting dots were gathered together and added to other dots which collectively make the final drawing.

Recently Pindell has increased the number of structural elements which inhabit the picture plane. She incorporates not only the dots but also hair, board slats, color pigment, the material from which the dots are punched and other remains which she places randomly on and throughout two-dimensional drawings and three-dimensional grids. The three-dimensional grid is more dominant since it acts as a structural linkage between the architectonic formations created by the protruding boards and dots as in *Untitled #88, 1977* (fig. 49). In this work the surface areas become more dense since the sculptural qualities seem to challenge the restrictions of the plexi-glass boundaries. Arrested movement and sustained rhythms abound as the drawing

48. **HOWARDENA PINDELL.** *Untitled #4. 1973*

appears to be frozen in time, possibly capable of expansion and release without notification.

In *Untitled #83* (pl. 12) a tension and depth are qualified by the intermingled interrelating forms. Sparkles have been included as they seemingly "wink," tease and provoke underlying optical surprises, catching and throwing light from within the art object's confines. This depth, these sparkles, the order and implied disorder provide the mysteries and secrets in Pindell's world. The optical activity which occurs forces the viewer to look, re-examine and reassess as he/she tries to ascertain the total imagery and physical properties of the work. Questioning and uncertainty become common visual effects. The work appears almost ephemeral in its visual presentation as the forms play within and without an assortment of remains.

Pindell's recent canvases employ this same quality of surprise and secret. An equal visual suspense is created as the color dots bleed into textural non- and monochromatic fields. She continues her assortment of remain materials to build on the textural quality and visual characteristics of the works. Her concern for the quality of materials becomes more pronounced as she arranges and rearranges their potential effects when placed beside, between and in juxtaposition to one another.

During 1977 the grid of the canvas has become the canvas itself. Making patchwork quilts from square-cut canvases she continues to obliterate the perceptual dominance of the grid by the build-up of paint and textural devices on its surfaces.

Since 1975 Pindell has developed a series of works, Video Drawings. Continuing her concern for order and disorder she randomly draws her arrow and number system on a piece of acetate which is then adhered to a video screen. Turning on the video and choosing the stations and programs at random, she shoots thirty-five millimeter photographs through the transparent acetate surface. By crumpling the acetate or moving the camera when shooting, she is able to vary the resulting effects of motion, vibration and distortion.

In *Video Drawing: Swimming Series, 1976,* (fig. 50) the juxtaposition of arrows and numbers increases the blurred moving appearance of the background, providing visual maps and interpretation to the form and future movement of the calves, ankles and feet. Order and disorder are rampant as focal points are suggested and dispelled.

Pindell's concern for diagramming thought, relative

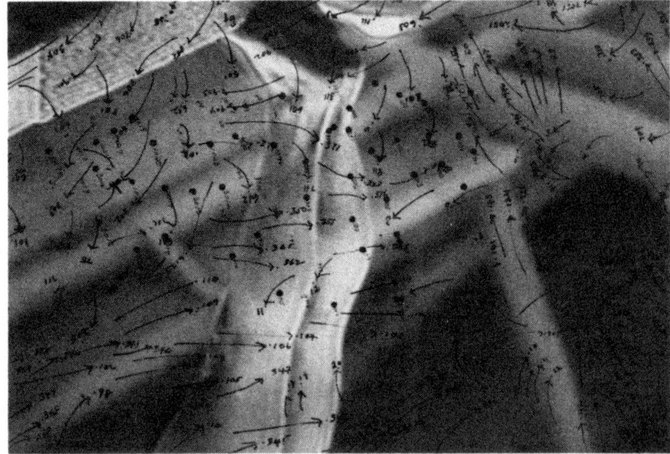

50. HOWARDENA PINDELL. *Video Drawing: Swiming Series. 1976*

positions, order and disorder and the mystical and ritual suggests an infectious obsession. One is able to examine the individual elements constituting a contextural whole in order to discern his/her potential ability to notably understand and affect the conditions in which he/she exists.

Self-communication, -understanding, -pleasing and -exploration form the solipsist and esoteric attitude of Banerjee. Exploring the nature of ancient, non-western and modern phenomena, Banerjee involves himself with the context meanings and understandings of man's interrelationships with self and environs. He focuses this attention directly on self as he constantly analyzes his relative position to external stimuli and conditions.

Banerjee is concerned with nature; the basic and most fundamental conditions of existence. By examining the properties of nature, he perceives its contradictions, its disorder, incident, happenstance, its control, order and habit. Primarily utilizing organic materials, he creates two- and three-dimensional works whose imagery is based on the visual translation of the states and conditions of natural phenomena.

During the 1960s Banerjee's canvases were influenced by Abstract Expressionist process and imagery (fig. 51). Overall gesture and color were achieved as suggestive geometric

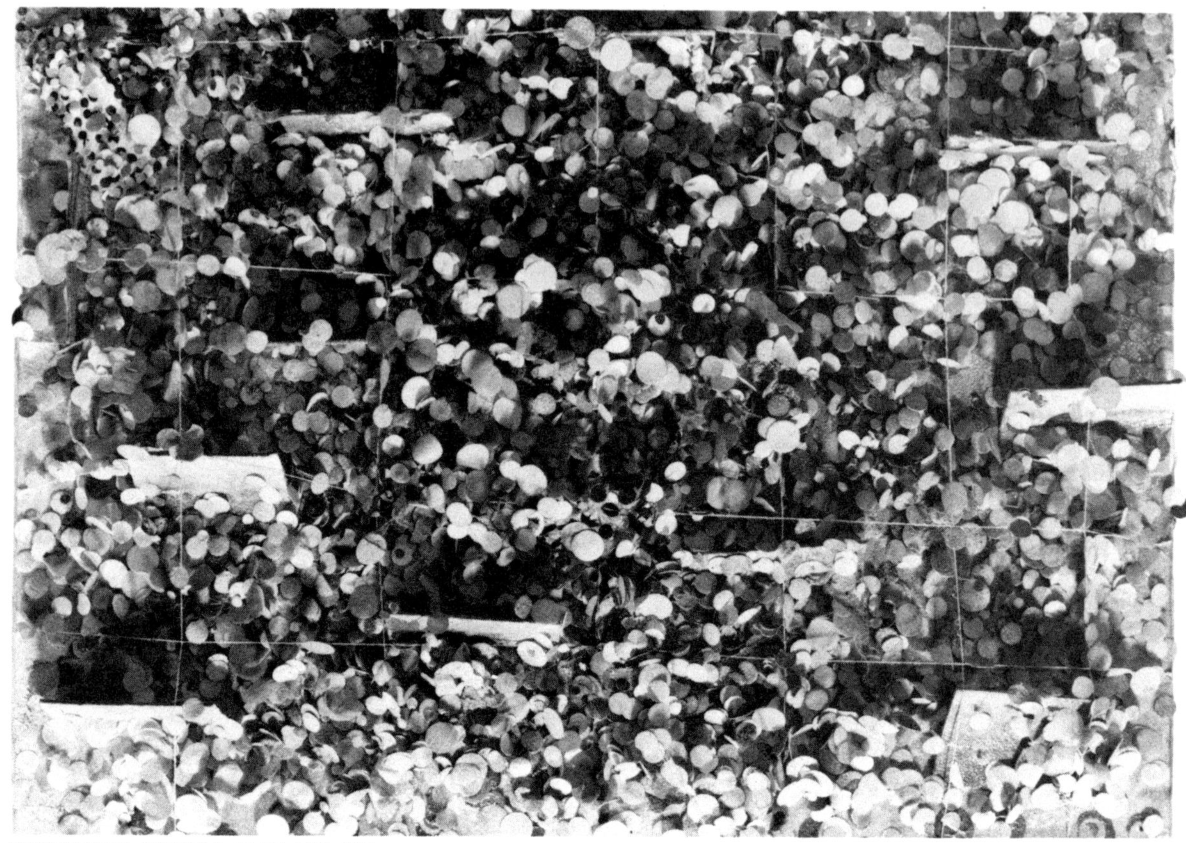

49. HOWARDENA PINDELL. *Untitled #88. 1977*

forms floated through an atmospheric ground of accidental drips, strokes and splattered color. By 1968 origami (which becomes a recurrent element in his compositions) was placed on the canvas surface. Based on geometric shapes, origami replaced the floating color forms since the overall use of canvas was reduced, and solid background color areas emerged (fig. 52). Canvas texture is achieved through the build-up of materials which are painted onto the canvas providing three-dimensional effects. These surface protrusions act as devices for depth, irregularly jutting on and off of the canvas surface. Grids and diagonals are drawn on the foreground acting as indicators defining and clarifying space and direction. By the early 1970s the division and distinctions between fore- and backgrounds were clarified. Origami and mixed-media surfaces began to dominate the focal point. Certain expressionistic and color-field elements were maintained utilized generally to provide a spontaneous contradiction to the methodical spatial delineations occurring on the foreground.

In 1972 the canvases return to an overall use of space and surface. This time, however, the imagery is dominated by mixed-media and origami collage painted and attached to the surface. Gestural color marks and brush strokes are superimposed by broken and continuous diagonal lines reenforced by horizontal origami folds. In these canvases Banerjee begins to explore his use of fumage.[55] Staining the surface with smoke-forms created by gestural movements, he controls the dense and wide bands which surround the central imagery. Reducing this imagery to a single form, generally a triangular or rectangle origami structure, the visual interest focuses on the textures which exist in the picture frame. Primarily the spatial divisions were delineated through these textures; the canvas painted solid and smooth; the origami, either of newsprint, paper, or cloth; and the fumage. The various textures provide a tactile quality to the work since the viewer is enticed by the dense and massive seduction of the smoke, intrigued by the intricacies of the fold and printed matter of the origami and repelled by the cool flat surfaced background.

Initially, Banerjee's use of fumage lacked the control necessary to achieve varying degrees of intensities, hues or texture. By 1974 after extensive investigation of the types of smoke and their resulting visual effects when applied as stain to the canvas, Banerjee was able to create what appeared to be a minimal painted surface that was contradicted by subtle changes in the stained areas. An oil stain which he applied in earlier canvases became more prominent acting as the illusionary shadow or depth of the surface.

Fumage, origami-collage, oil stain, lead, colored pencils and house paints are Banerjee's primary materials. His fumage-stain technique is intricate and immediate as the natural properties of the smoke require automatic application. Initially, Banerjee composes his imagery mentally. Placing the canvas on the floor and exposing it to natural light he then marks off the shaped areas on the canvas that result from the shadows occurring from the sun's penetration through the window. He paints a solid ground of color on the canvas. Placing the canvas in various positions he begins his fumage staining. Varying the types of smoke, a

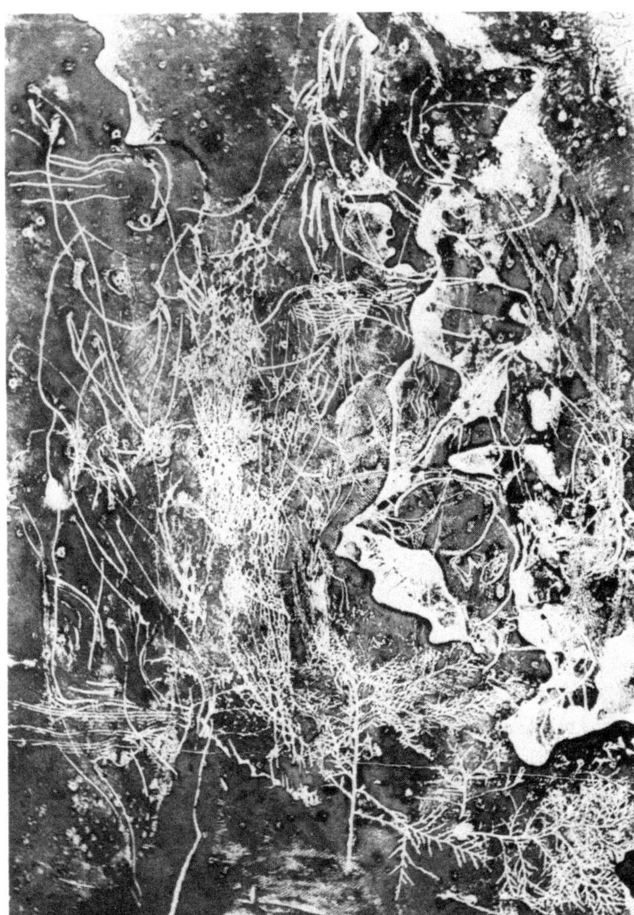

51. BANERJEE. *Characterscape. 1965*

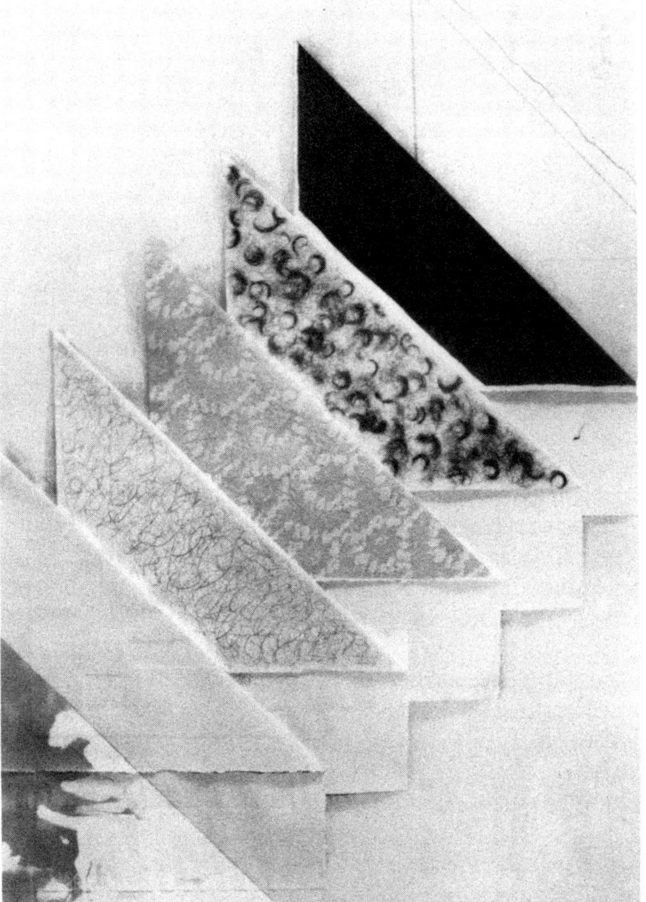

52. BANERJEE. *Diagonal Origamis*

diversity of textures, hues and densities are achieved.

By 1975 Banerjee returns to an overall use of space as origami, drawings, paint and fumage dominate the picture plane. Now the fumage was free to intermingle with the other objects and materials. Floating in and out, behind and in front, its textural and tonal qualities provide added tactile effects.

In the canvases of 1976 (pl. 13) the origami floats, seemingly in isolation, on the picture plane. His application of materials assist in this illusionistic effect as he heightens visual contradictions through composition and form.

Banerjee's works on paper employ origami-collage, fumage and drawing (fig. 53). Working from the shadows cast by plants and their structure he creates lyrical, loose structural images which are met with geometric lines and folds. The exactness of the geometric and grid system is contradicted by the fumage and origami forms. A call and answer dialogue is established between the images. Banerjee, to emphasize the contradictions and cohabitation of order and disorder, exposes the accident and continues his use of spontaneous-like motion as his calligraphic notations consciously jerk out of focus from exacting grid structures. The balance altered, his images become unpredictable, teasing and taunting, challenging any attempts to classify or confine them.

". . . (A) true work of art is a mirror of an artists' soul. The pain, agony, the joy, the feelings, in general life's metamorphosis in search of newness, pedagogic and cognative thoughts . . . All these are my inner echoes, foundation and it transmits to my inner soul and creative intellect, and it inspires me tremendously to work wisely."[56]

The private world of Noah Jemison is provocative, humorous, playful, sensuous, sensitive, tactile, sexual, serious, isolated, communal, physical and spiritual. It is the context nature in which these elements are combined that provides the viewer with an intimate and autobiographical sketch of the artist's mental, emotional and metaphysical being. Concerned with the physical, psychological and emotive qualities of forms, Jemison appears to conjure perfect relationships among these properties through an automatic and unconscious process meeting in a mental and physical ritual of naked exposure. This convention of metaphysical and physical properties results in anthropomorphic forms which seemingly possess a variety of spiritual attributes and sensibilities.

Initially, Jemison's works during the 1960s were Social Realist commentaries on social and political ideologies and conditions. In the early 1970s he began to abstract his work, producing shaped hard-edged and minimal canvases in which he employed his first use of the encaustic technique. By altering the traditional approach to this process, Jemison bleached his wax to insure pure color, eliminating any chance of imperfection in his intended palette. He apprenticed himself to the technique completely learning its idiosyncrasies. Structured and methodical, Jemison approached these canvases as technical studies. Method and structure were the primary objectives as he analyzed and dissected spatial and linear relationship in order to control the necessary elements to achieve an intended perceptual response. Muted colors dominated his palette during this time since geometric form, line and color became the primary content of the surfaces.

As his technical control over the encaustic medium and structural imagery became secured, Jemison began a series of watercolors. Contradicting the visual properties of the canvas, these watercolors consisted of free-flowing unrestricted abstracted figures placed often in distorted yet referential settings. While the realistic presentation of form had been discarded, the rendering of these figures still implies a loose association with external subject matter and stimuli. As these watercolors evolved, the forms became freer. Association with subject matter or an external stimuli were eliminated. The settings were further broken down by abstraction into atmospheric notations which implied a floor and ceiling hierarchy in which the figures performed. The works maintained their narrative quality. This was achieved through the gestural form and movement of the figures in space rather than content based on recognizable subject matter or implied realistic settings.

By the mid 1970s, having perfected his technique and control of the encaustic method, Jemison opened up his canvases. No longer restricted to geometric content, loose and expansive forms evolved. Large biomorphic beings dominated the entire picture frame, defined by interwoven areas or sections of color. *Pandora's Box* was one of the first canvases executed in this manner. Using bleached bee's wax and powdered pigment Jemison stained the entire surface of his unprimed canvas with color. Delineations of forms were achieved through linear gestures of broad solid colors which lay on top of the enmeshed atmospheric field of free-flowing encaustic mixtures. In *Flower Eaters,* Jemison began to expose unprimed canvas areas

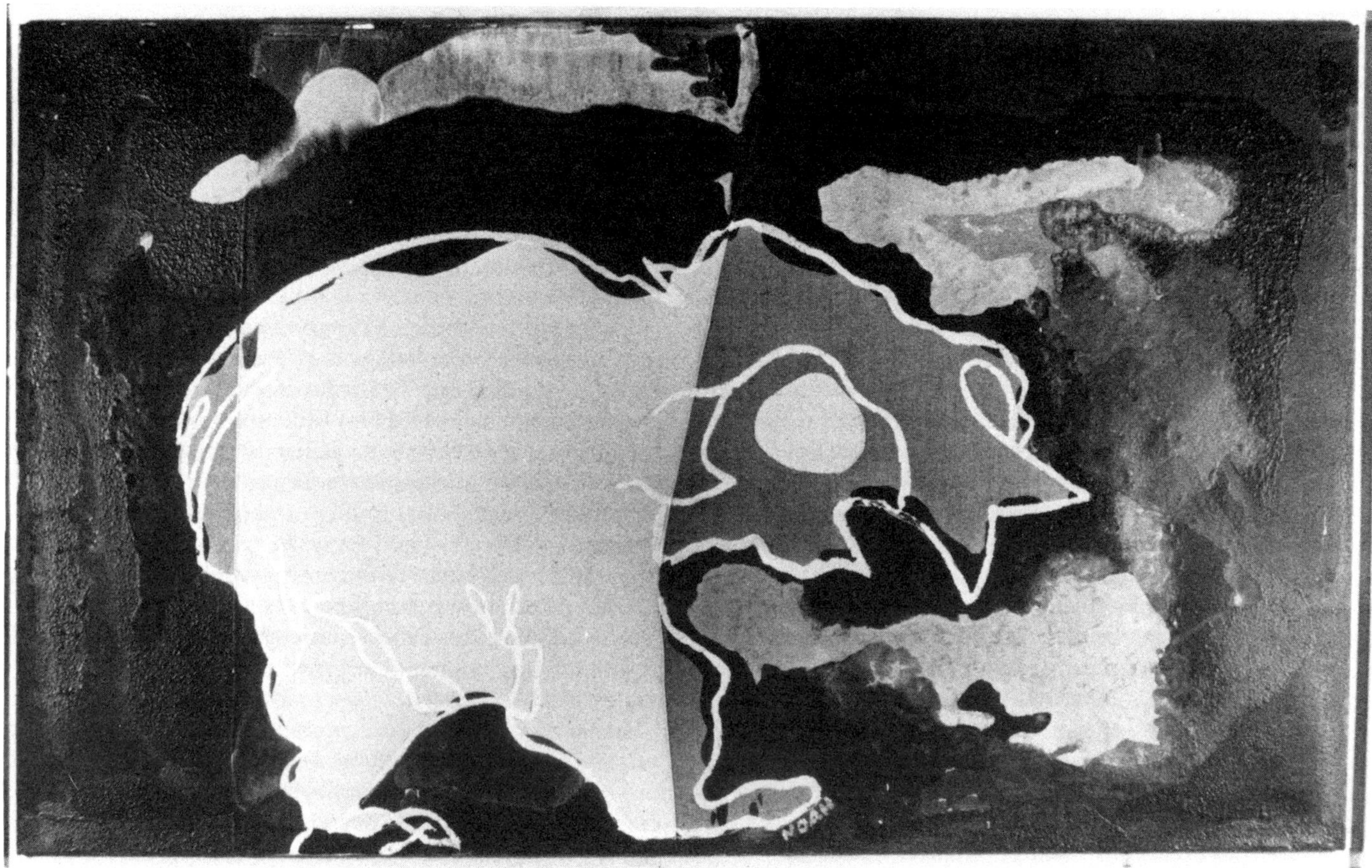

54. NOAH JEMISON. *Walking Through the Universe (Happy as a Pig in Shit) 1977*

around the canvas' border. A huge biomorphic form is created through this free-flow application of wax. Its internal structure was achieved by repeating the delineations created with large white gestural strokes of gesso.

Fascinated by the positive and negative spatial interplay suggested in *Flower Eaters,* Jemison executes *There's A Bone in the Biscuit.* Seemingly child-like forms float between large areas of exposed canvas defining space and movement.

The forms in Jemison's watercolors during this period become anthropomorphic. Removing all traces of a background setting, they float in large areas of exposed paper. Each form is rendered in a gestural action as if talking, walking, dancing, laughing or meditating. The technical devices he achieved in the earlier canvases is apparent as he is able to masterfully control the internal flow of pigment while defining the external boundaries of the form with color lines. The contained fusion of color acts as an emotive element which teams with the gestural positioning of the figure to expose the characters of the form. Anthropomorphic forms begin to inhabit the surface as the play of positive and negative is continually emphasized.

Jemison's process is completely automatic. He does not begin with concept or an idea. The free-flow of the wax-pigment into the canvas surface provides the initial shape that the forms will eventually take. Unlike the spontaneity of the Abstract Expressionists, Jemison's automatism differs in attitude and intent. His primary concern is not the exposure of process or spontaneous expression, but rather a ritual in which he participates in order to go within himself and remove the conscious mind to get to the essence of what the imagery is going to convey. To him spontaneity is like " . . . dealing with life and not knowing what's going to happen in the next minute: in the painting."[57] Music becomes the transportation which takes him out of himself, allowing him to be a medium for external physical and spiritual forces.

Jemison and his art become one in this process. He is completely consumed by the materials and forms which are automatically exposed during the process. He becomes the viewer, only aware of the interaction of forms and content after the execution has been completed. "The work is so close to me that it's frightening . . . I discover things that I like, tidbits and gossip about myself from my art."[58]

The unconscious mind and being of Noah Jemison become more radically exposed in his works done during 1977. An almost total release from external conditions and human protocol have been dissolved as the works become grotesque, beautiful, funny and completely independent, dictating their nature, content and essence. These radically exposed anthropomorphics exude spiritual messages and knowledge as they float in unison or in isolation throughout the space. They peek, they taunt, they speak with their gestures becoming animated, as if Jemison has captured spirits in space and time that want momentary exposure.

In *Walking Through the Universe (Happy as a Pig in Shit), 1977* (fig. 54) Jemison returns to an overall use of the canvas. A transparent pig outlined by white gesso is superimposed on an expressionistic background, and made prominant by its unprimed canvas interior. Jemison begins to expand the elements defining the visual content by sewing shaped canvases together. The seams act as separations between the planes with illusion and depth further enhanced by the relative positioning of the forms to the seam. Thus, the pig appears to be walking from one dimension to another as the colored and non-chromatic canvases meet.

In *The Mythological Allegory of the Real Chumpy-Doo, 1977* (pl. 14) these seams become more apparent as colored and nonchromatic canvases are joined to divide this triptych into multiplanar levels. In addition to seams, Jemison expands on the frame. It no longer acts as the finished border but becomes a sculptural component in contrast to, yet enhancing the two-dimensions of the canvas. In this painting the tiers on the frame are varied sequentially from one frame of the triptych to the other.

In *Divorce, 1977* (pl. 15) Jemison returns to floating forms on unprimed canvas space. His imagery becomes melancholy as the distortions and interactions of the forms define their relative positions and relationship in an isolated and alienated atmosphere.

Jemison considers his art work hedonistic made for his own understanding and inner needs. "It's selfish, a vehicle for me to express (and define) myself . . . My art and I have become one . . . The forms are common, however, thus allowing the work to be used as a bouncing ball for all that view."[59]

Large acrylic canvases, ranging in size from four to ten feet, dominate the early works of Randy Williams from the late 1960s to the early 1970s. Incorporating formal elements of Hard-edge and Op, Williams focused on color spectrums defined by pastel horizontal bands. His primary concern during this period was the use of color in relational formats which evoke emotive and optical effects. These formats were prescribed by a catalog of predetermined formulas devised from a series of investigations exploring the effects of various combinations of color range, intensity and hue. These combinations then translated into formulas which became the basis for the compositional structure of each work.

Generally restricting his palette to variations of pink, yellow, green and blue, Williams extracts all but the elemental properties of color, achieving minimal or reductive results which focus exclusively on line and color interactions. The reductive quality is further enhanced by his flat application of paint, eliminating any textural or expressionistic suggestion. By varying the line or direction and width of each band, an illusionary fore- and background are achieved. Contrasting and seemingly spontaneous band assortments emerge from his combination of repetitive and non-repetitive color band. Thus, the band arrangement is not numerically sequenced nor are the size, length or width consistent throughout the total work.

Color and color arrangement become an essential component of his optical effects. The properties of each individual color when combined and placed side by side with the properties of another create an illusion of change and difference. Essentially, the same color intensity and hue, when placed in the context of another intensity and hue, will vary in optical effect depending on the color placement.

Color and color placement is further utilized to evoke emotive effects. While maintaining the same color, hue and intensity, repeating it throughout the canvas, Williams is able to provoke a variety of sensory perceptions by his relational formats. These effects indicate and imply a variance in color which only exists perceptually.

In addition to the concern for line and color relationships, movement becomes a prominent element in these works. Through implied and actual variations in line and color, the integration of thin lines between color bands accentuate illusionistic movement. These thin lined bands are often of a color different from the bands they connect. However, the incidental nature of their application, as well as the overall effect of their placement between wider bands, deemphasize their distinctions, making them almost imperceivable. As a result of the combinations of line, color and accents, a symmetrical force is achieved, exposed through the relational patterns established by similar and contrasting elements.

During this period, Williams worked on a series of drawings which combined the skeletal structure of the human figure with geometric line drawings placed in the fore- and background areas. Employing a similar system of symmetry and use of subtle devices noted in the paintings, Williams focused on form similarities between the triangles, squares, circles and rectangles occurring in the skeletal and line drawings. Color is used merely as an accent in the first drawings. As these works developed he began to incorporate subway maps and watercolor bands. The lined shape becomes solid form and the subway maps become the connector between repetitive shapes.

The drawn lines become the connecting factor between the shapes in each form rather than color. The skeleton is distorted through elongated poses and its space is restricted by lines placed on the immediate outer edges of the figure. Williams, then adding Color Aid paper and cutting into the surface paper, juxtaposed white with color backings. The Color Aid is used also as geometric collage accents on the surface.

The technical and exacting aspects of these drawings are assisted by his usage of a compass. This allowed the hard-edge quality of the paintings to be translated to the drawings. Dissections of the skeletal form led to further abstraction where the drawn line and collage became more prominant. His use of maps was extended to include the use of discarded pages from books and paper debris.

Williams' use of discards and debris in these drawings which date through 1975 predict his transition into Contextural Art. Fascinated with the book concept, he began his first book series, but continued his investigation of form and color interactions. Utilizing standard drawing books, he cut geometric forms into the pages. A number of white on white, form on form works resulted. Retaining this format, he began adding color paper. Initially attaching the color to the pages within the confines of the book, he allowed them to extend beyond the original pages, causing a shaped and irregular frame or defining boundary. These works became expansive in size ranging from four-by-four inches to four-by-five feet. Cutting and assembling color and construction paper on the pages, exacting geometric lines continuously occur. Through the usage of color paper, Williams continued his investigation of color interactions and transitions. In these works, pastel is replaced by vivid, warm earth colors. Blank books were substituted for printed books. Limiting the amount of color paper, this series of books concentrated more subtly on the relations between line and form since he utilized the print size and design as a guide to cut and formulate geometric shapes.

Moving from the horizontal bands and pastel palettes of earlier canvases, Williams, between 1975 and 1976, worked on a series which he termed "Music." Using music as the catalyst for these works, he began to visually construct the melodic and textural elements of jazz and classical music. Unlike the works of Dowell which primarily focus on the compositional structure of sound, Williams concentrates

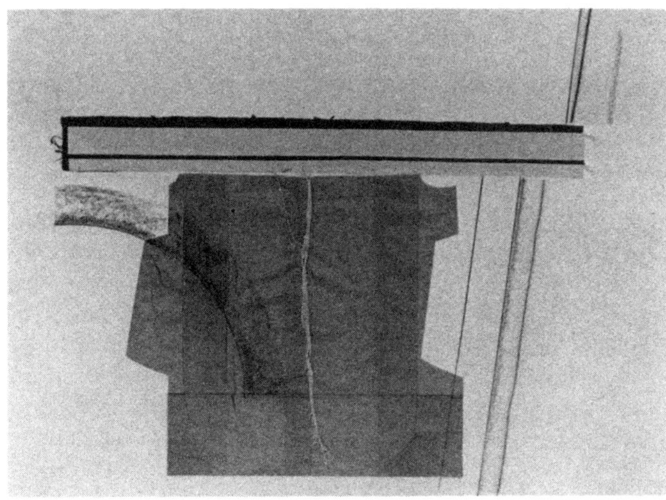

55. RANDY WILLIAMS. *Untitled October #1. 1977*

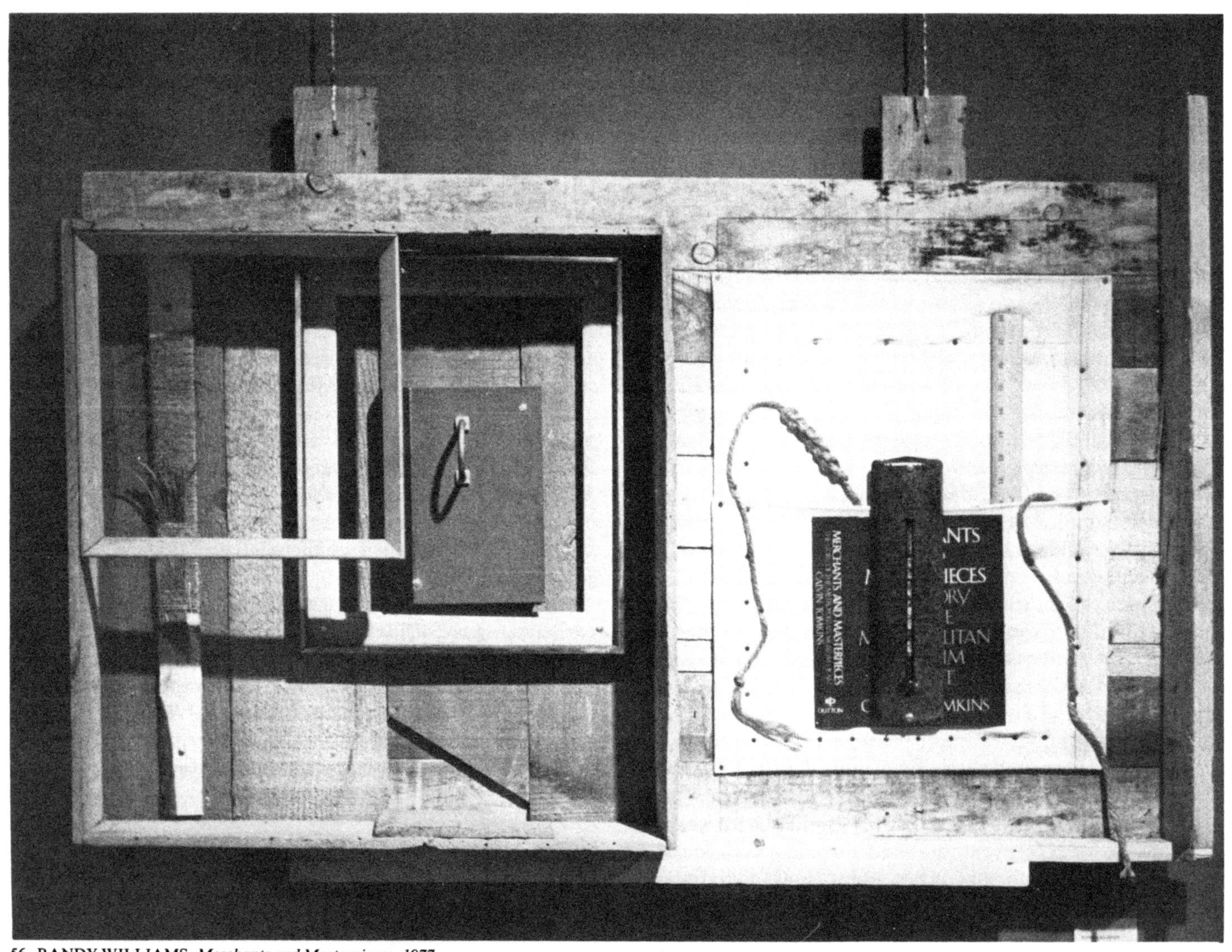

56. RANDY WILLIAMS. *Merchants and Masterpieces. 1977*

on its impressions. No longer utilizing an illusionistic fore- and background, he defined a separation between the two, juxtaposing lyrical and hard-edge forms on a solid background. Initially, the fore- and background planes of these works were developed with the same color but were contrasted by changing the register. As these works developed, three layers came into existence—a front, middle and back —defined, again, by changing the register of the color. The top layer forms engulf all but the corners and sides of the surface areas. By flatly applying the paint and building it up, Williams suggests a continuation of his cut-out method of extraction. The negative and positive become superimposed as the fore- and background become intermingled, almost contradicting what appears to be an apparent division of planes. The integrity of each interconnected form is maintained through his thin line device of the implied and actual connecting parts. In *Study for Music IV, 1976,* Williams begins to expand his palette. Utilizing four colors, and for the first time employing a dark ground, the forms become more distinct. Accents are not only line but color markings which divert visual attention away from any implied focal point. *Blues People, 1976,* marked Williams' return to subtle variances in hue changes while adding an interplay between contrasting colors. These contrasts are restricted to interconnecting lines which dissect the background and middle layers. The background is no longer solid, but rather is built from almost undistinguishable color changes. Since late 1976, Williams has completely eliminated pastels, limiting his palette to investigations of color differentiations through subtle tonal interplays. Reductive to the point of implying minimalism Williams again relies on accents in order to challenge these subtleties with bold and contrasting line areas. While synthesizing the elements of his earlier works, he accentuates the overt, balancing it with the subtle. He developed layer upon layer of shape and form, extracting and adding color as a means of delineating the areas. His transitions are quiet. A green rectangle will suddenly surprise the viewer then disappear into an orange line and dark surrounding background. A square will suddenly be transformed into a curve without the slightest indication, leading the viewer further and further into layers of visual activity.

His drawings have developed into works on paper consisting of shapes and forms made from debris and remains. He continues his concern for the geometric utilizing found paper bags, burlap, string and watercolor. Williams works from the natural folds of the bag to define and dissect shapes and forms. Maintaining the repetitive element, he provides alternate modes of perception of simple shapes. The circle is perceived from its positive and negative properties. The rectangle is intersected by triangles, repeated, distorted, altered and perceptually transformed.

Presently Williams' works on paper fuse lyrical and architectural line into textural compositions. By increasing the amount of the remains material, a tactile quality is achieved which subtlely plays on the separation and distinction of protruding and receding planes. In *Untitled, October #1, 1977,* (fig. 55) Williams focuses on a central vertical axis (string) which is perceptually strengthened by the off-center line markings which lie under and above the dissecting horizontal band. The graphite texture echoes the natural texture of the bag providing contrast to the flat paper ground, and accentuating the textured canvas strip. The balance of horizontal and vertical is achieved through repetition of the horizontal by the top fold of the bag. Perceptually, the work would appear perfectly in balance but through seemingly accidental strands of thread protruding from the edge of the canvas strip as well as the isolated graphite diagonal marking to the lower right side of the picture plane, Williams deliberately upsets this balance allowing accident and happenstance to exist.

Williams' book series since 1976 is his most obvious involvements in Contexturalism. No longer a progressional subordinate to his two-dimensional illusionistic explorations into form and space, these three-dimensional structures embody pages and covers of contextural relationships and definitions.

In *Merchants and Masterpieces, 1977* (fig. 56) strong compositional elements are balanced by contextural content and meaning. The history of art is assessed as the book's contents are bound shut, and the relationships between the significant and the frivolous are displayed. The process of creation is illuminated by the used paint brush, rope and the measuring stick. All acting as compositional reenforcements to the interplay of horizontal and vertical pulls, they exude a significance that overpowers the suppressed contents of the book. The act and the process are escalated as documentation is subjugated to a subordinate position.

In *L'Art Abstrait, 1977* (fig. 57) Williams pits irony and wit against an artistic commentary which alludes to abstraction in a mocking yet supportive way. Incorporating

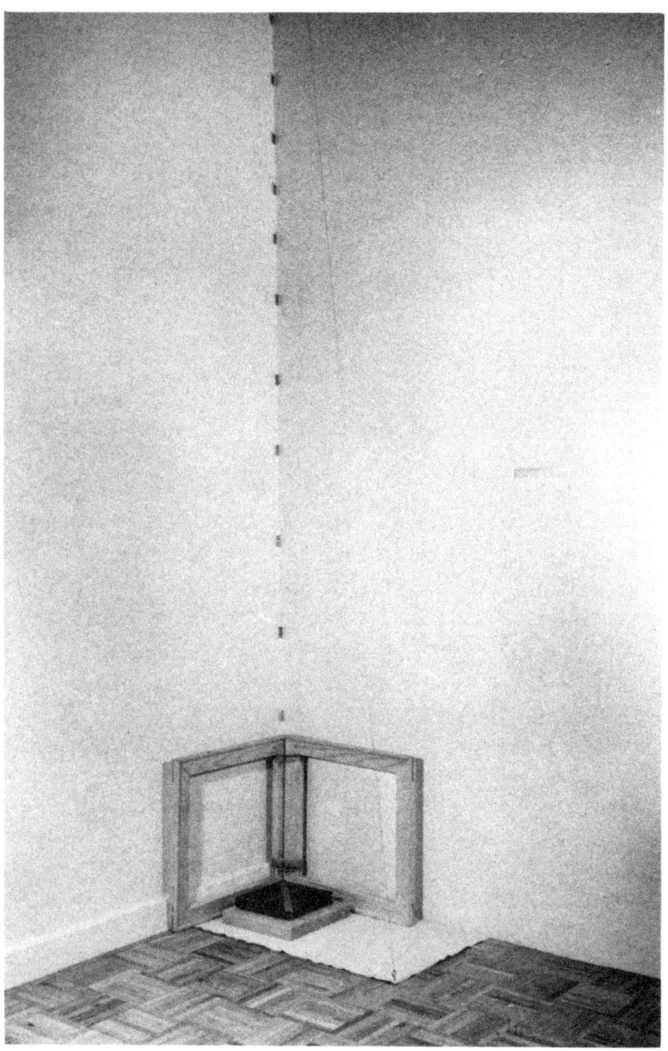

58. RANDY WILLIAMS. *Homage to the Edge of a Corner. 1977*

lottery tickets, hooks, cloth and wood, this open-faced construction intricately contains a Dadaist reaction to art as it assesses abstraction and the seeming impasse which is occurring. "This particular art object—at once ferocious, elegant, mocking and beautiful—has something very precious about it."[60] Its visual definition, while seemingly reactionary, provides inroads allowing further expansion, exploration and investigation of abstract development.

Williams breaks from contained constructions in *Homage to the Edge of a Corner, 1977* (fig. 58) incorporating space and environment as components within the total composition. A jarring tactile sensation is created by the vertical corner row of razor blades. The corner is accentuated further by the open frames which intersect at right angles forming a structural interplay between the triangle and square. These are repeated by the video cover and its wooden stand in which a ruler is placed covered by exposed razor blades. This sits on a carpet of cloth which is used again as a square and triangular hybrid achieved by extending a thin fishing wire from its corner to the ceiling at the section where ceiling and wall intersect. Corners and illusions of corners are constantly repeated.

In *Twenty-Three Years of Black Art, 1977* (pl. 16) Williams produces a direct and poignant statement in which a more obvious and blatant display of contextural meaning and definition takes precedence over his subtle devices. The catalog, *Two Hundred Years Of Black American Art,* is pressed and concealed behind a metal black shoe-shine stand. A washboard occupies the upper portion of the covering for the John Coltrane album it conceals. Textural effects of the washboard's surface are balanced by a wood-textured overcasing at the bottom. The bolts used to compress and conceal add an additional feel of weight to this structure as the contradictions are exposed through contextural definition; reality declared, illusions dispelled.

AFRO-AMERICAN ARTISTS WORKING IN THE ABSTRACT CONTINUUM

BOWLING, Frank
BROWN, Marvin
CLARK, Ed
CONWILL, Houston
DOWELL, John
EDWARDS, Mel
EVERSLEY, Fred
GILLIAM, Sam
HAMMONS, David
HUGHES, Manuel
JACKSON, Suzanne
JEMISON, Noah
LITTLE, James
LOVING, Al
NENGUDI, Senga
PINDELL, Howardena
PIPER, Adrian
SAAR, Betye
SAUNDERS, Raymond
SUTTON, Sharon
THOMAS, Alma
WILLIAMS, Randy
WILLIAMS, William T.

COLOR PLATES

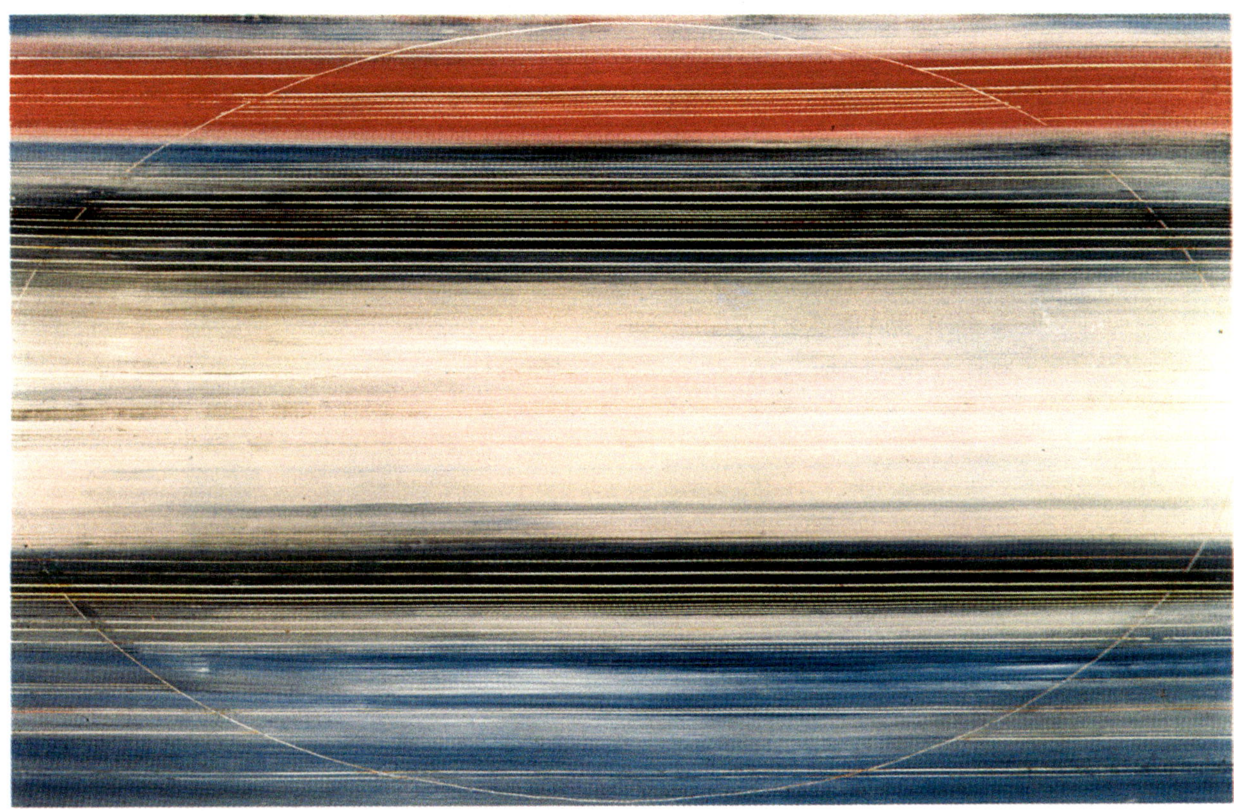

1. ED CLARK. *Integrated Oval, I. 1972*

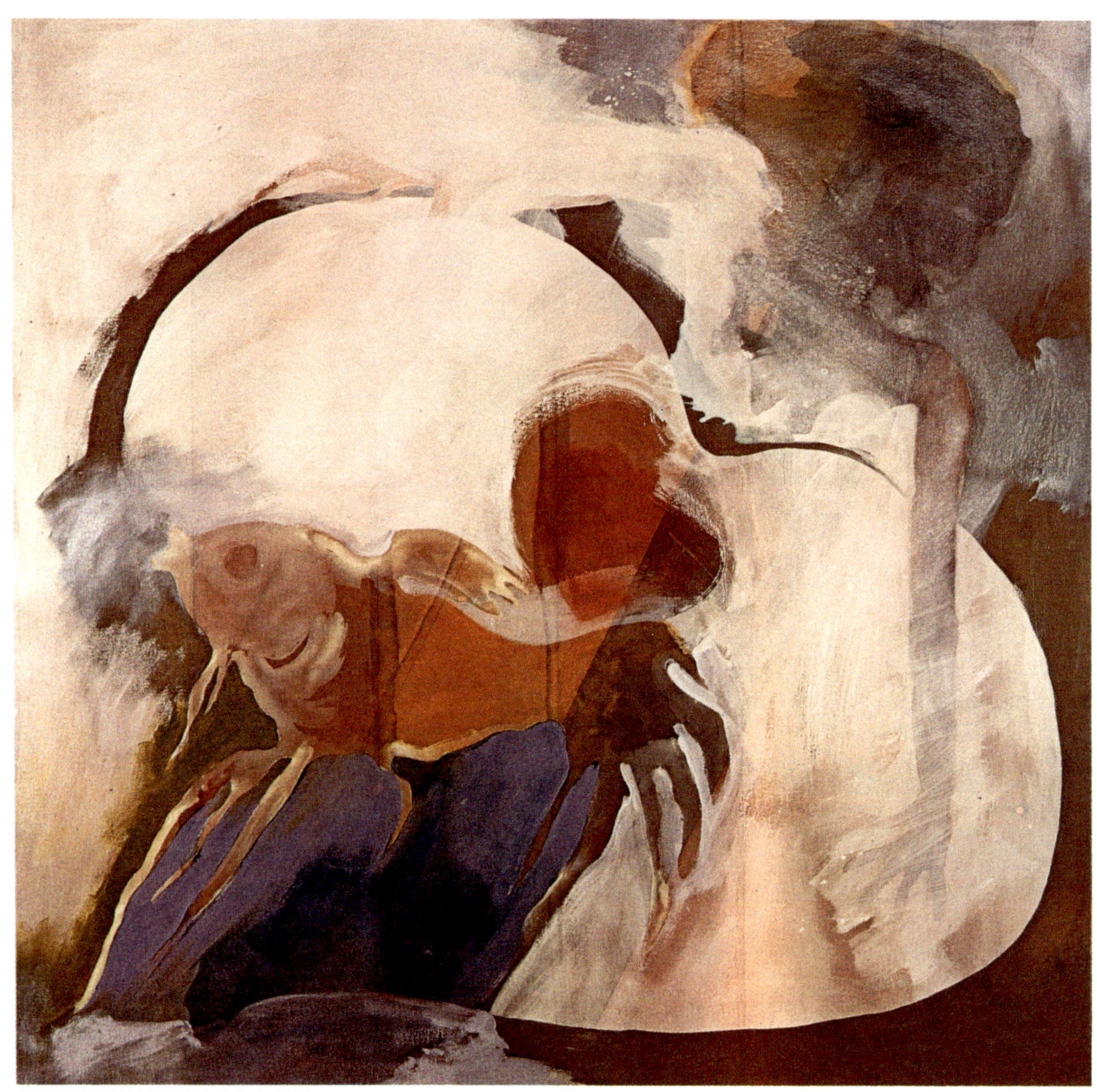

2. SUZANNE JACKSON. *Splash. 1976*

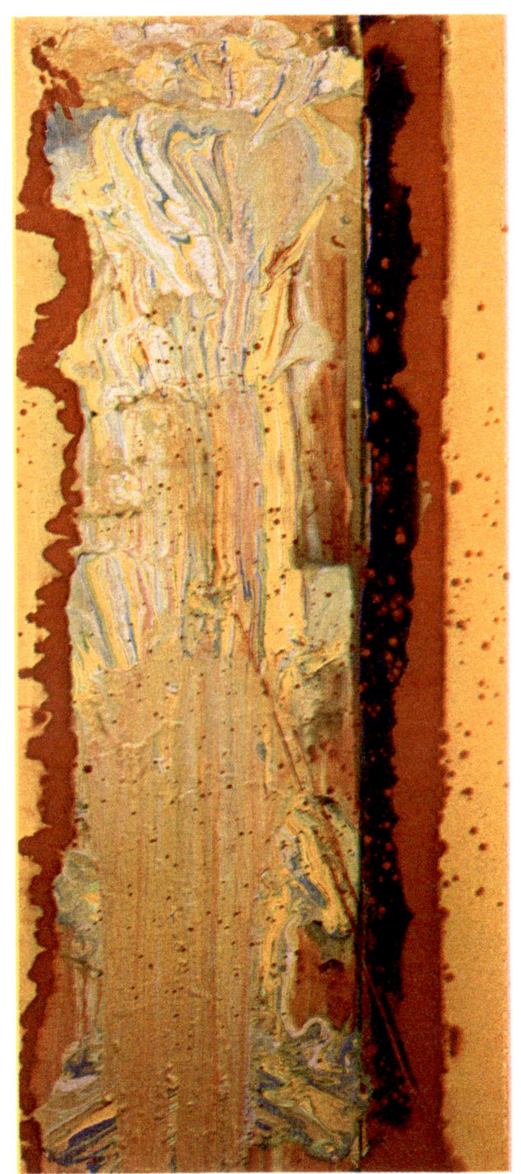

3. FRANK BOWLING. *Valley. 1977*

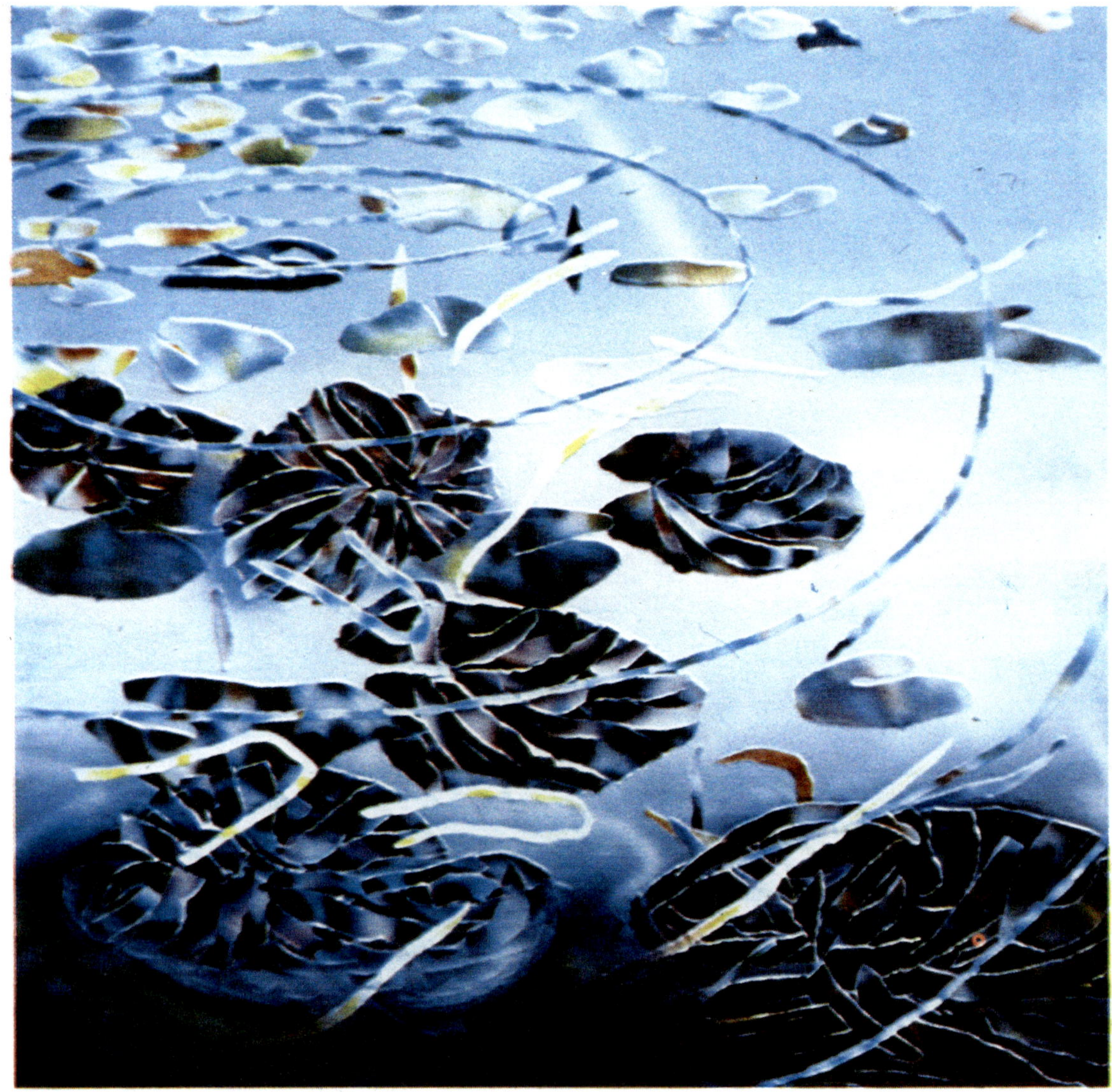

4. AL LOVING. *Untitled. 1977*

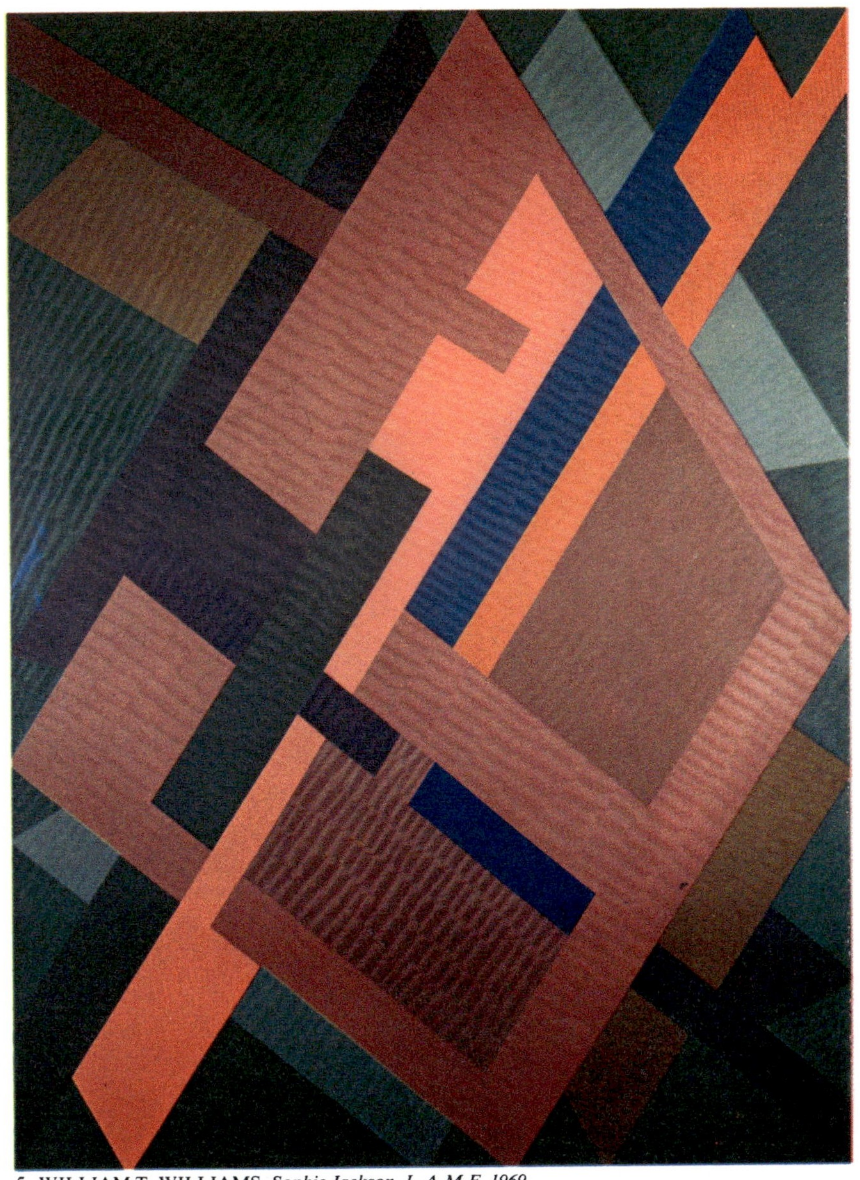

5. WILLIAM T. WILLIAMS. *Sophie Jackson, L.A.M.F. 1969*

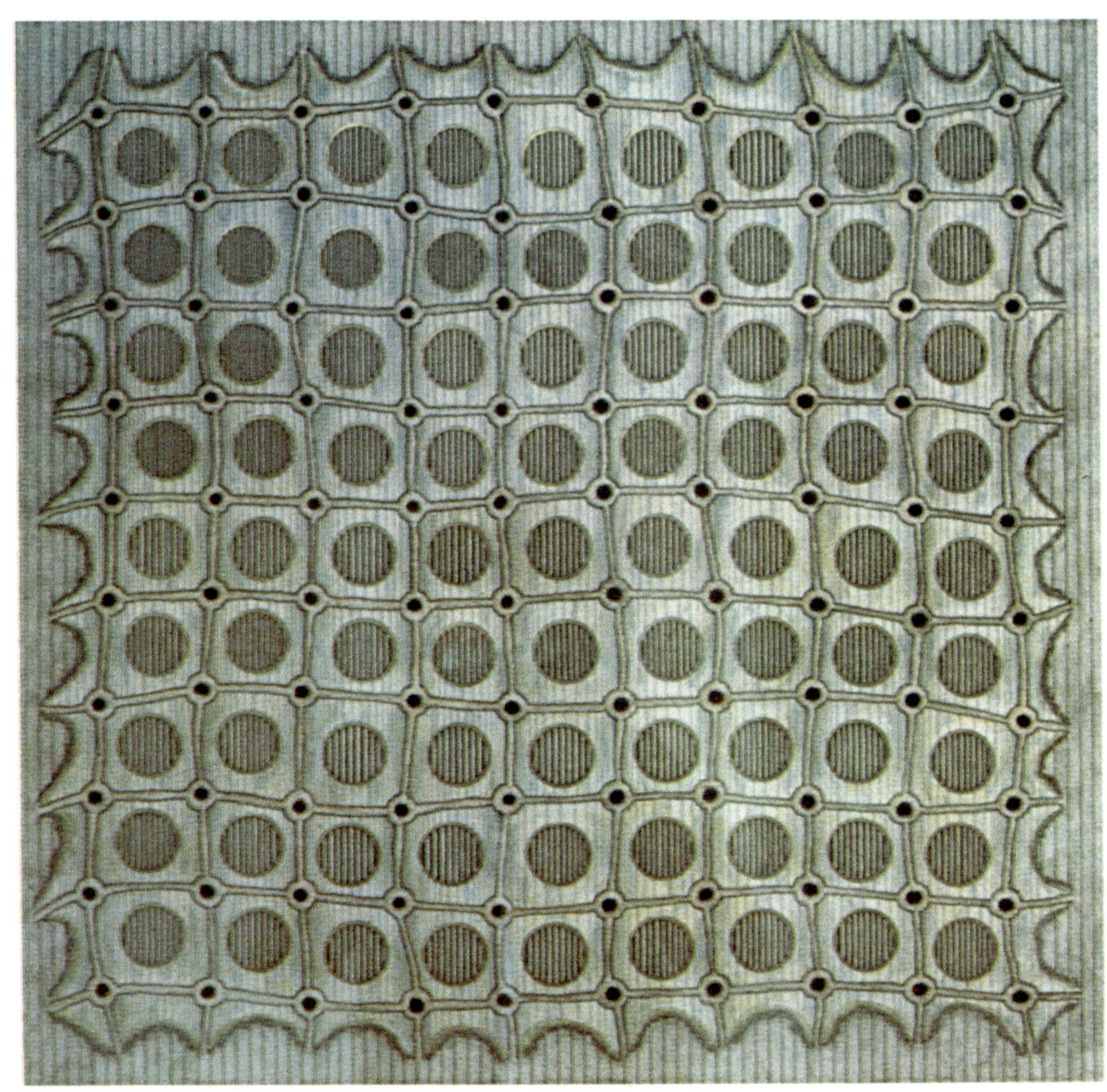

6. SHARON SUTTON. *Fading of that Fabulous Olden Lady. 1977*

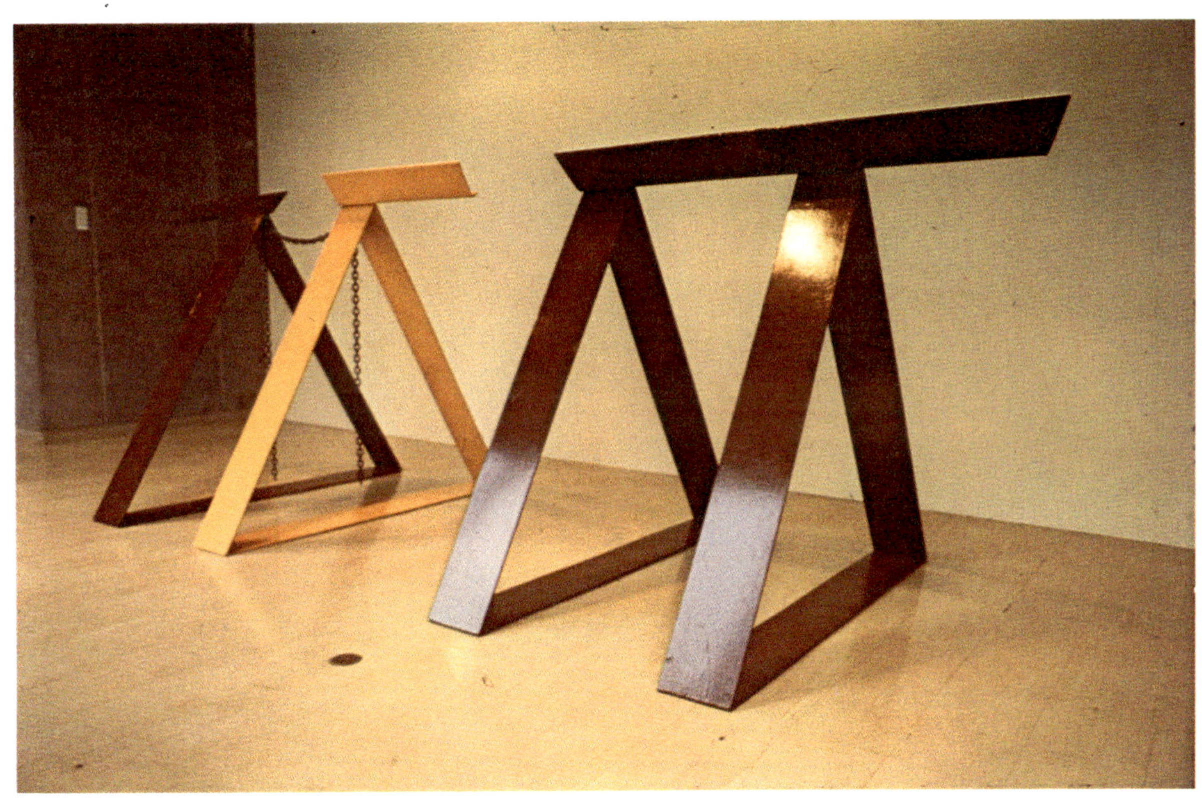

7. MEL EDWARDS. *Try, try. 1973*

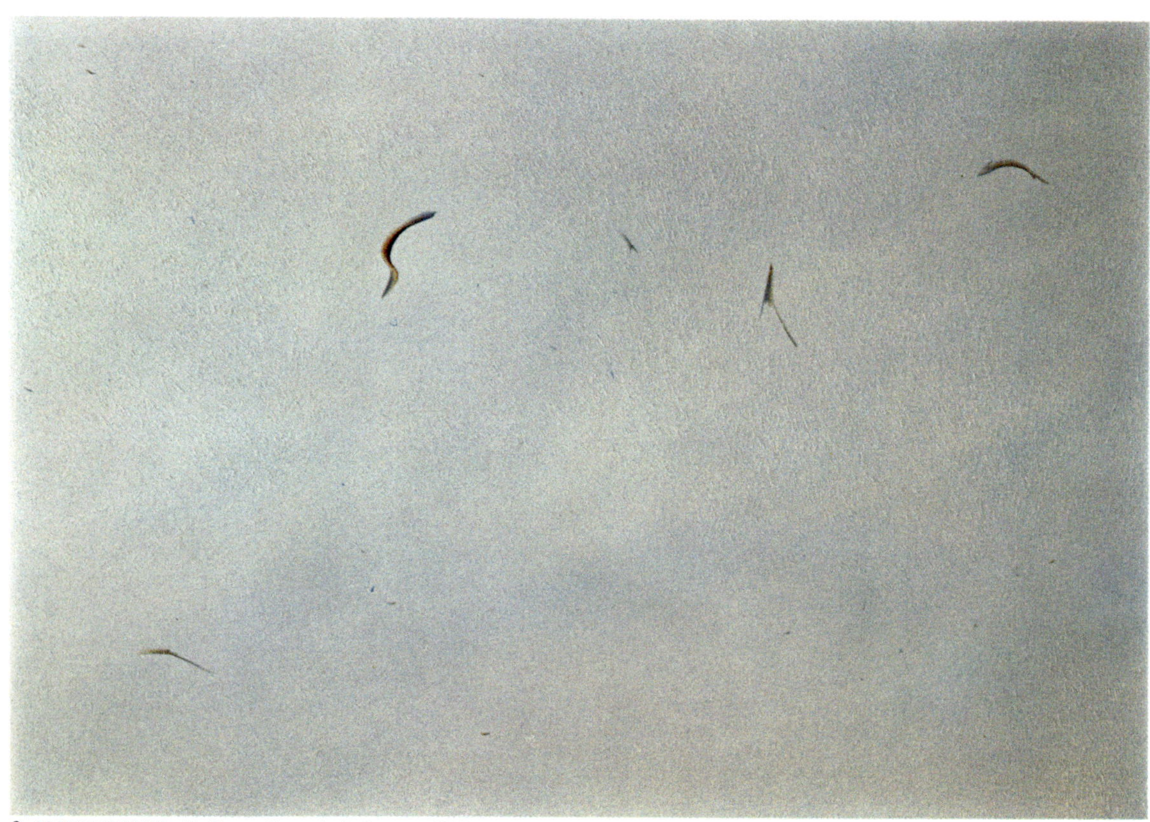

8. JOHN DOWELL. *To Dance Yesterday's Dreams. 1977*

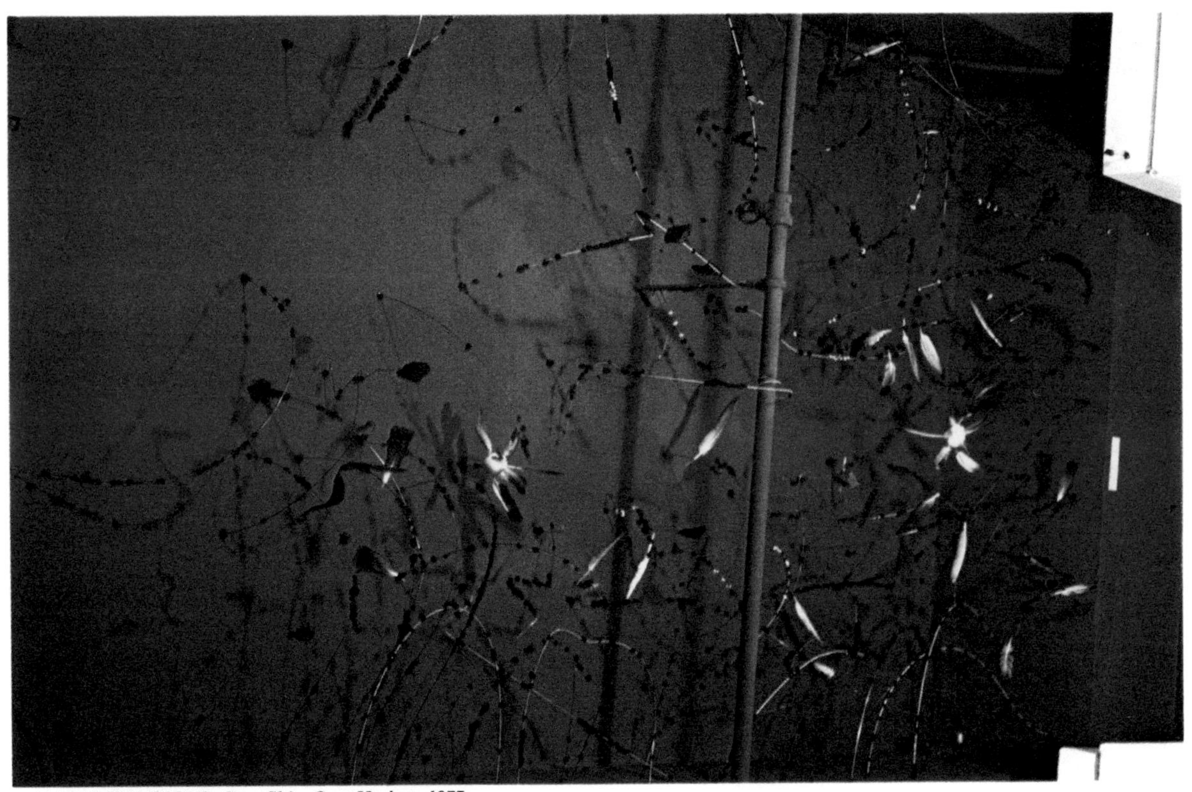

9. DAVID HAMMONS. *Gray Skies Over Harlem. 1977*

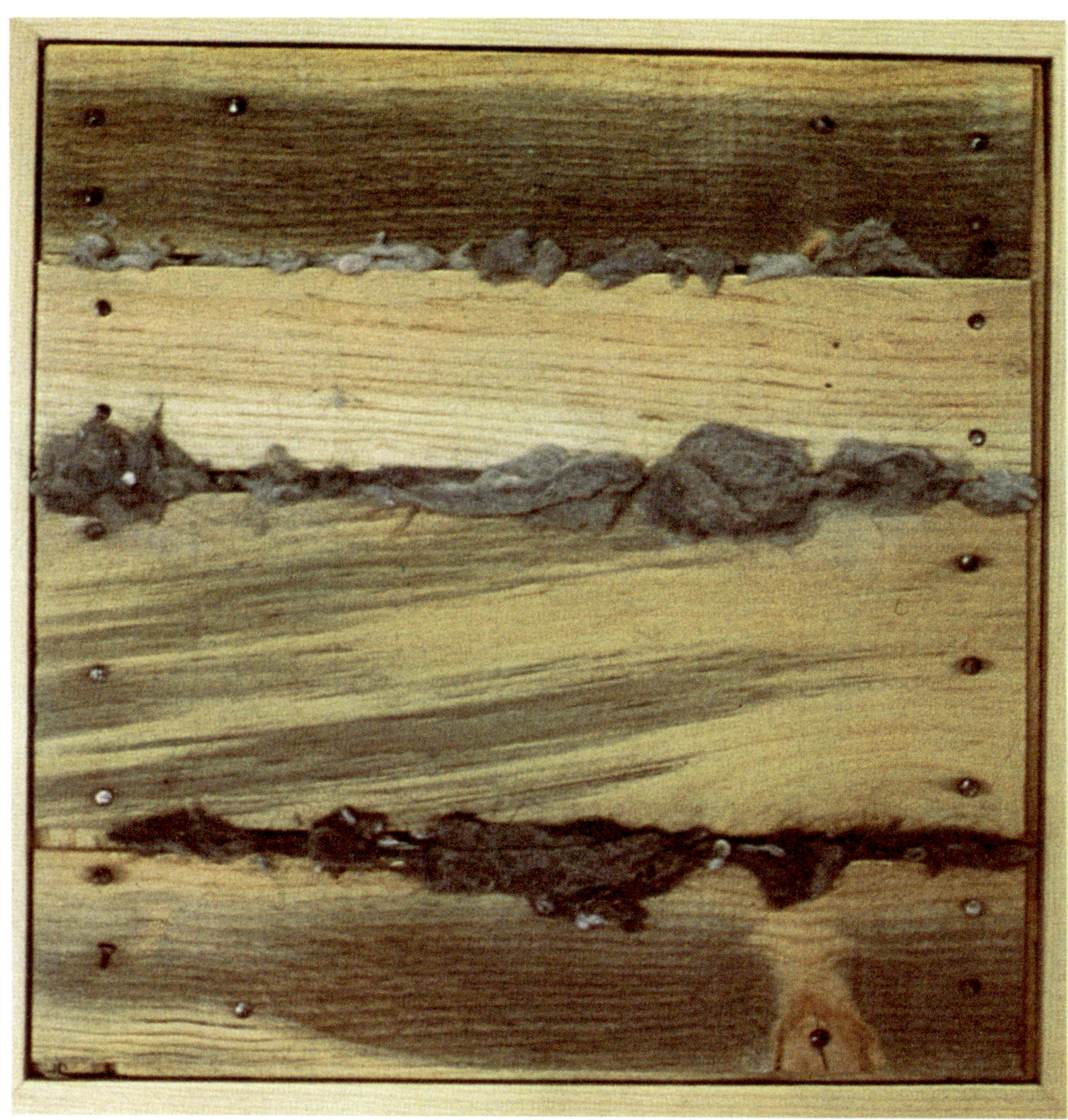

10. WENDY WARD EHLERS. *Traces. 1974*

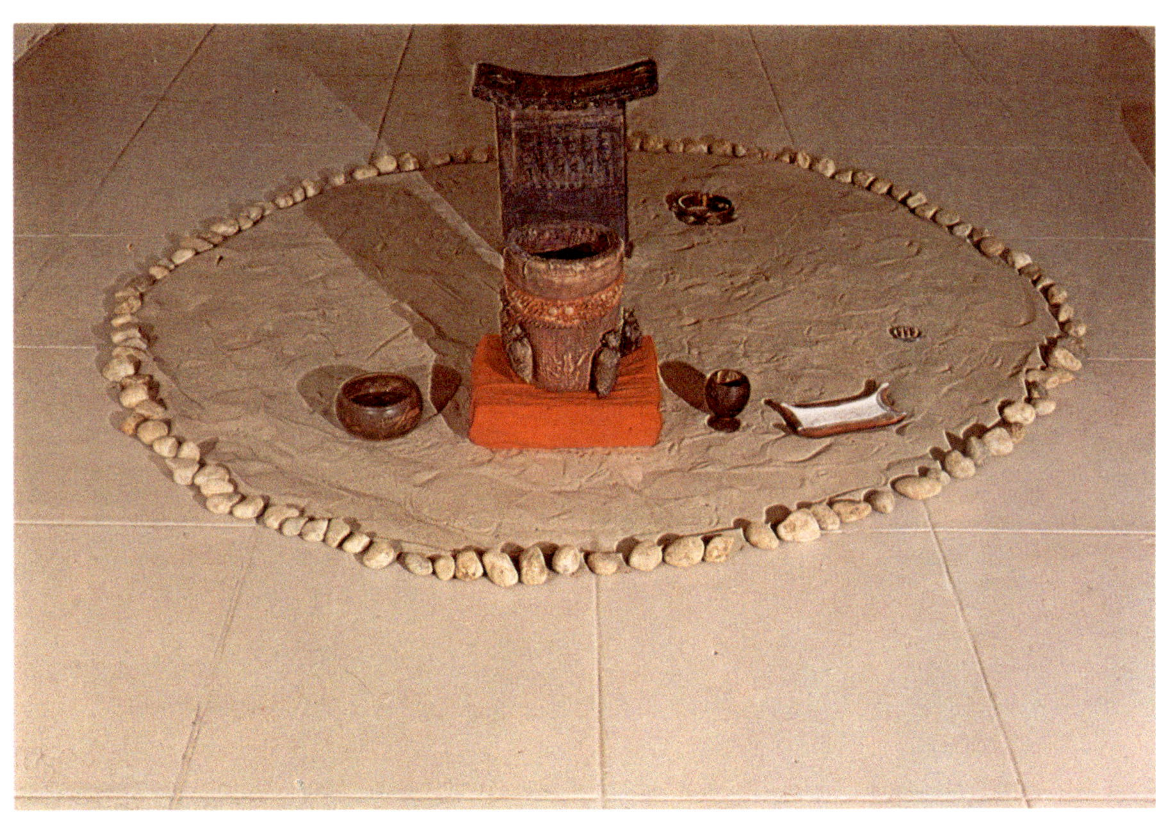

11. HOUSTON CONWILL. *Juju (installation). 1977*

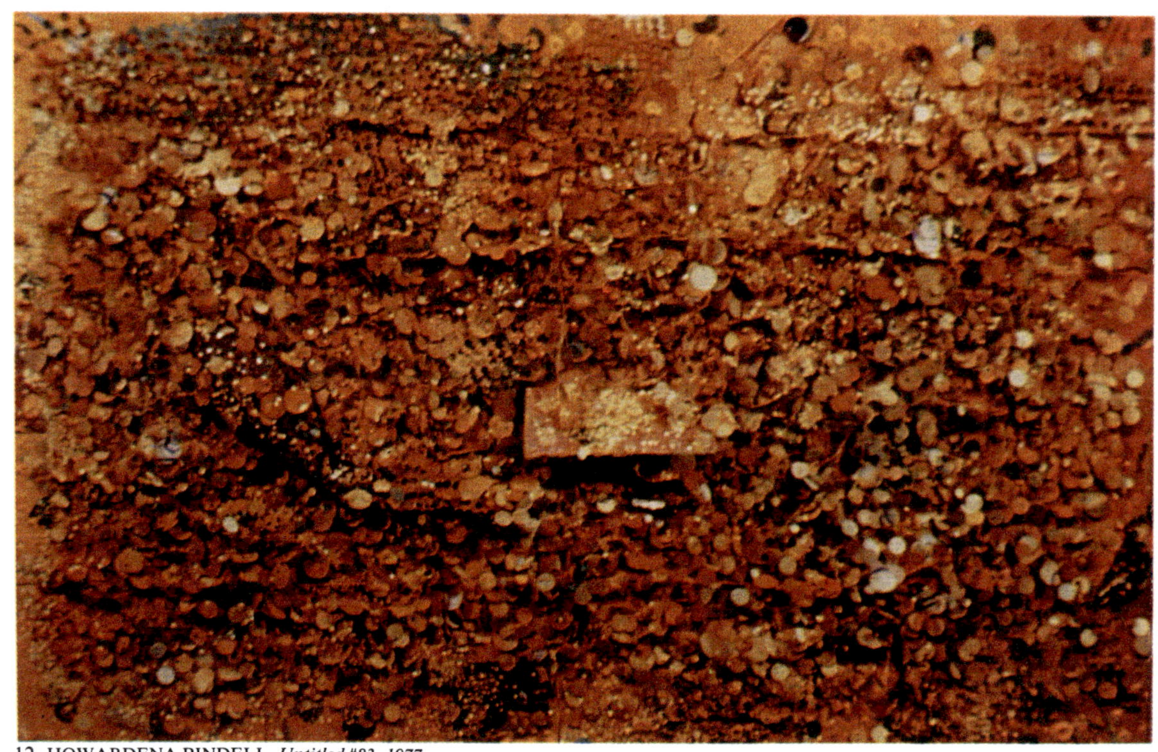

12. HOWARDENA PINDELL. *Untitled #83. 1977*

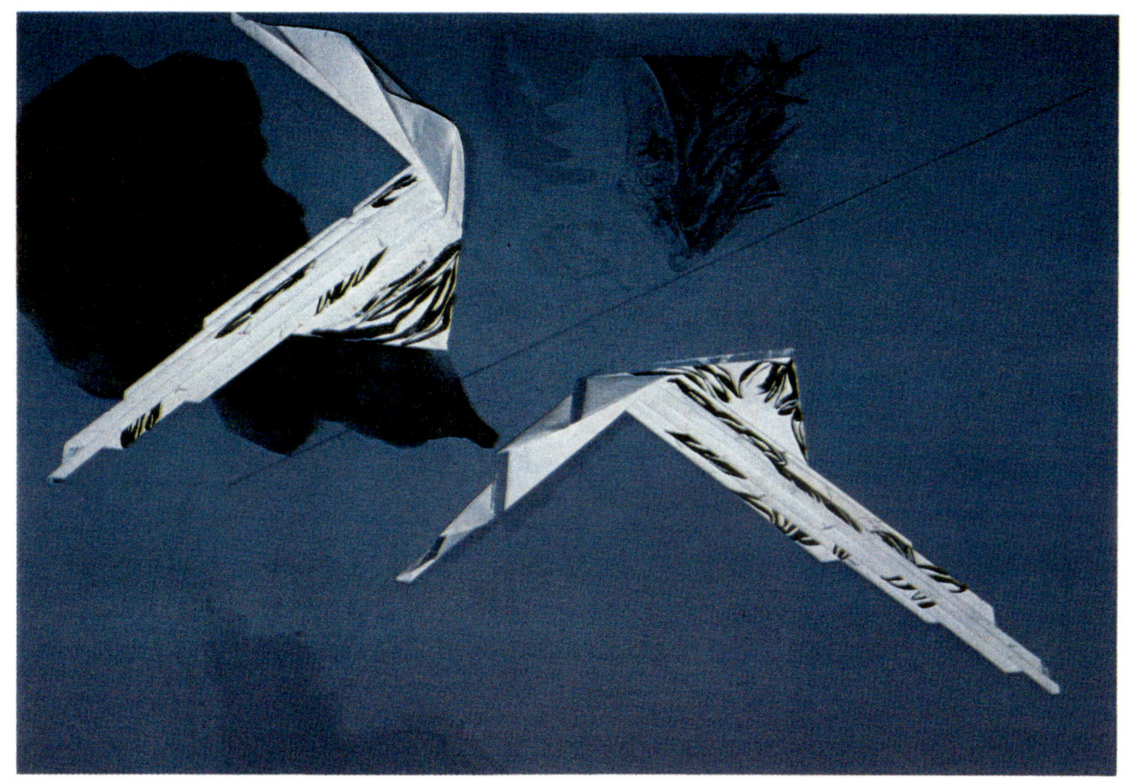

13. BANERJEE. *Fern Horns Hundred. 1976*

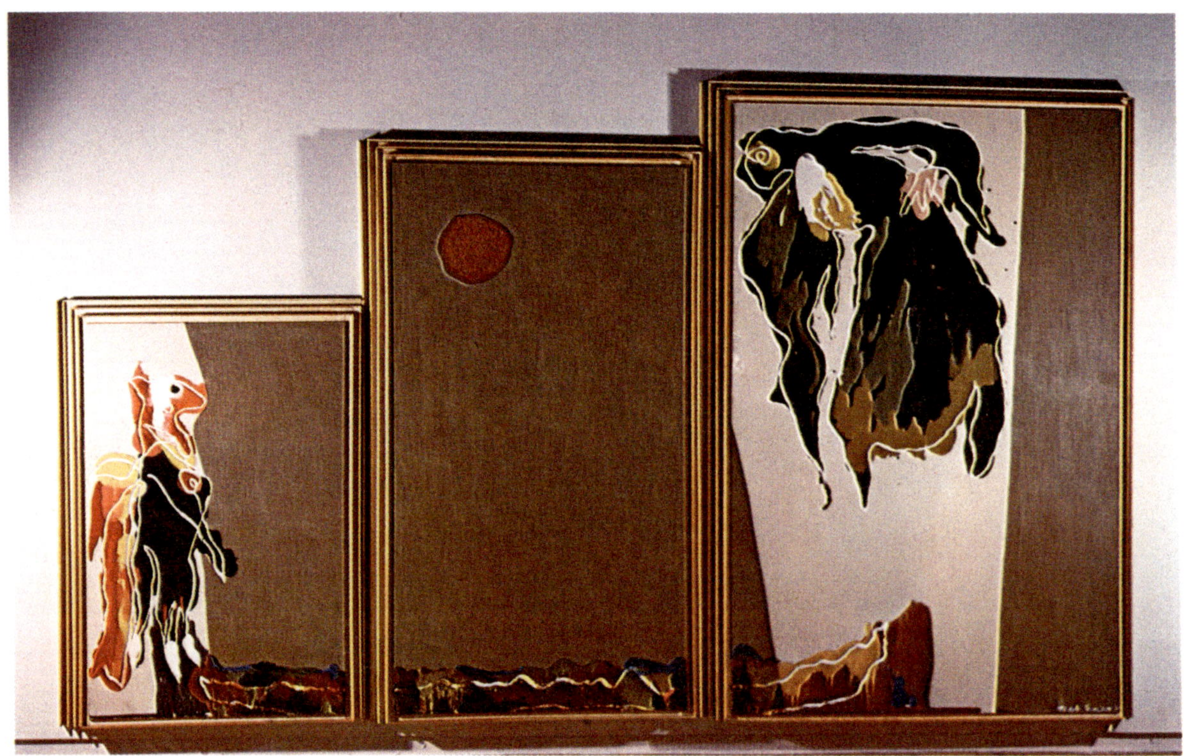

14. NOAH JEMISON. *The Mythological Allegory of the Real Chumpy-Doo. 1977*

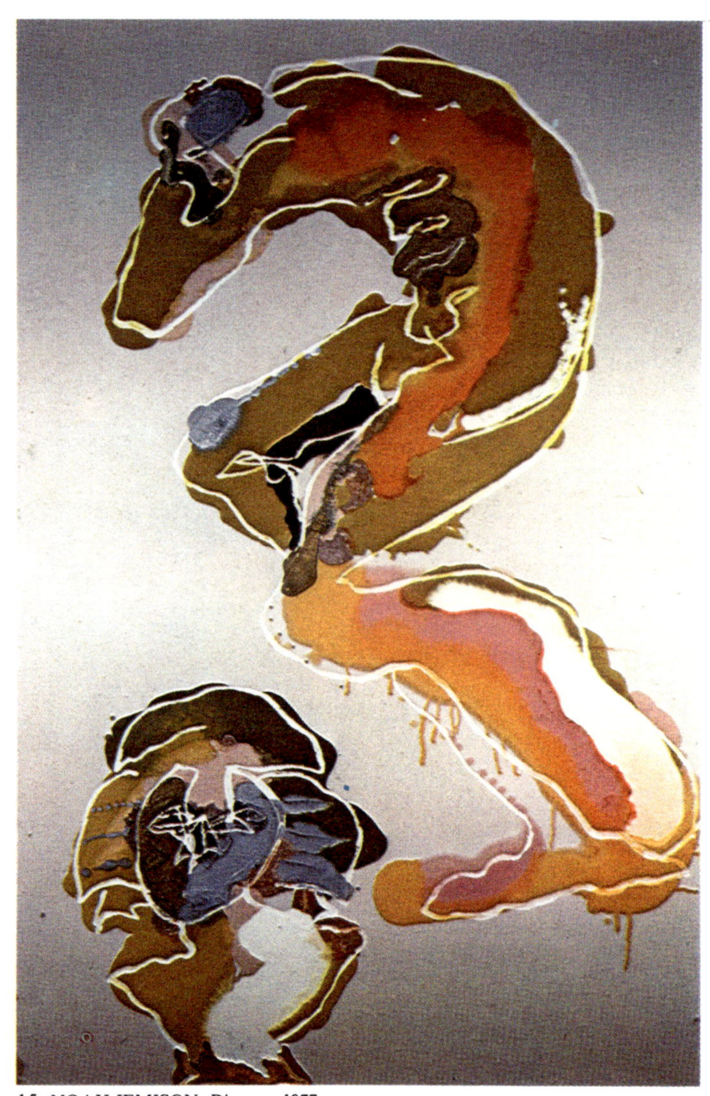

15. NOAH JEMISON. *Divorce. 1977*

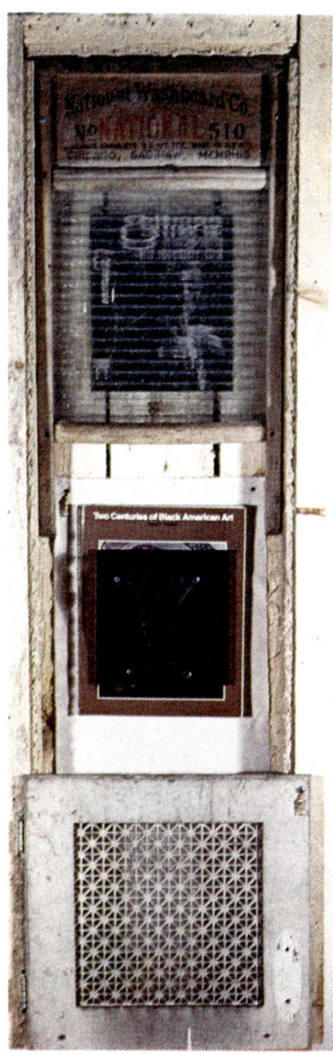

16. RANDY WILLIAMS. *Twenty-Three Years of Black American Art. 1977*

CONTEXTURES: AN AFTERWORD

Let's go back to the beginning. On the front cover of this book, Senga Nengudi poses for the camera, expressionless. Alone in her studio against a blank wall and enveloped by a paper tarp with traces of splattered paint and a necklace around her neck, Nengudi is both a figure and an abstraction. She wears a scrap of nylon mesh pantyhose on her head; the stockings' two legs hang down from her eye sockets. You can see her nose emerging from a masklike form.

How do we know that this ocher orange publication is a Black book without knowing the race of the masked figure? Nengudi's costume, with its references to the Japanese Noh theater and West African dance traditions she studied, synthesizes a range of cultural traditions through the folds, pendants, and cavities that mediate her body and ours.[1] In one glance, this catalog cover telegraphs the desegregationist stakes of the subsequent hundred-plus pages of *Contextures*—the sole book published by Linda Goode Byrant's maverick Just Above Midtown gallery (a.k.a. JAM) during its twelve-year run from 1974 to 1986. Although the inside back cover of the book states that "this catalogue was prepared for the exhibition, The Afro-American Artists in the Abstract Continuum of American Art: 1945-1977," that exhibition never came to pass. Like many aspirations at Just Above Midtown, the statement of intent was just as important as its actualization. The right to a future is not given but asserted.

Published independently from any individual show, *Contextures* provided a map for the JAM cosmos. A treatise on artists working in abstraction and other nonrepresentational forms, the book is composed of three long-form essays and a suite of colored plates. It describes and historicizes an interracial group of artists working together since the early 1970s on the East and West Coasts, under the influence of a globally inflected Black culture. Littered with interview quotes, the texts prioritize the artists' voices, portraying them as experts in their own work, theorists unto themselves. The book's title, a portmanteau of "context" and "textures," signaled the importance of place and materials for these artists, who often used remains—leftovers and scraps—from prior performances or actions.

Contextures' emphasis on remains was especially important for the gallery's approach to racial desegregation, signaling a departure from the autonomy and decontextualization that had characterized traditionally white approaches to abstraction and concretism. In their introductory essay, Linda Goode Bryant and Marcy S. Philips painstakingly diagram the history of abstraction as it had been defined by white art historians. Then they depart from that model, describing the artists associated with their neologism as "determining and clarifying the inherent properties of art" and going outside of art's margins "in order to incorporate it within the context of external phenomena."[2] For Contexturalists, "the marginal elements will maintain their nature and integrity throughout this incorporation."[3] In this definition, I hear a series of declarative statements untethered from fixed racial classification: *"Art" has always existed beyond what museums categorize under that name. And even if what Contexturalists make is integrated into this thing called "art," Contexturalists will remain outside of that category.*

This earlier definition of art required the separation of art's materials from its context, as well as the metaphorical separation of the individual maker from hers. JAM offered an alternative. Let's take as an example our cover image, *Costume Study for Mesh Mirage* (1977).[4] It seems to be unmistakably Nengudi—but might her authorial self be the mirage to which its title refers? It bears the trace of her signature material: the pantyhose that hang and distend in her celebrated *R.S.V.P.* sculptures. But while it features her body faced front, directly toward the camera and now the reader, Nengudi remains obscured, object-like; only her nose is visible, through which she takes in and exhales breath.

Around the same time that Nengudi was experimenting with paper and pantyhose around her studio, she made another work, *Air Propo* (1981), in which she also used breath as a material, inhaling repeatedly before buckling backward in a gesture of release. In 2022, when I organized a retrospective exhibition about JAM at MoMA, I asked her about her work from this period and how she used breath as a tool. Nengudi told me, "I was trying to become a conduit for something else . . . losing the self and allowing this other spirit to come through."[5] Many cultures have associated breath with spirit, claiming the organs through which it passes—the mouth, the nose—as the threshold to other people and their potential passage through us.[6] Recently, writer Kevin Adonis Browne has described breathing as "the beginning" and "as soliloquy [. . .] which echoes the vast chorus."[7]

The sublimation of the individual maker that Nengudi described as "losing the self" was a hallmark of Just Above Midtown. The gallery's acronym—JAM—was intentionally evocative of the improvisatory sessions in which jazz ensembles make music, suggesting a community of collaborators and conspirators with whom the gallery maintained an intimate dialogue. Many of those same artists and culture bearers are represented in the pages of this publication—Randy Williams, Banerjee, Suzanne Jackson, David Hammons, Susan Fitzsimmons, Wendy Ward Ehlers, Howardena Pindell, Noah Jemison, and others. The same diffusion of authorship also extended to the book's authors, Goode Bryant and Philips, who had been in conversation since they met at City College of New York at the beginning of the 1970s. With *Contextures*, they once again joined forces to write into the void of critical commentary on Black artists. Philips researched and promoted the book, while Goode Bryant came up with its concept. Like Nengudi's private performance for the camera, their study was an exercise in the uncanny intimacy of collectivity, in which what appears to be a singular figure embodies the force of many more.

Even if the show meant to accompany this catalog never went down, plenty of other events did, including numerous fundraisers to finance the gallery's publication of the title, and book parties to continue raising money and bringing people together on both coasts. Dawoud Bey documented one of those parties, held on the same day as the opening of artist Houston Conwill's performance *Notes of a Griot* in March 1978. In one photograph, Goode Bryant and Philips proudly leaf through the book; in another, Conwill whispers something into Goode Bryant's ear. Remains persist in these glimpses of shared pride and friendly intimacy, just as they do through the republication of the book you now hold in your hands.

Thomas T. (Jean) Lax
February 2024

1. I am indebted to Eric Booker for his analysis of *Contextures*. Eric Booker, "A Book Party for *Contextures*," in *Just Above Midtown: Changing Spaces*, ed. Thomas (T.) Jean Lax and Lilia Rocio Taboada (New York: Museum of Modern Art, 2022), 40.
2. Linda Goode Bryant and Marcy S. Philips, *Contextures* (New York: Just Above Midtown, 1978), 39.
3. Goode Bryant and Philips, 39.
4. This work was later renamed *Study for Mesh Mirage* and dated 1978.
5. Thomas (T.) Jean Lax, "Up in the Air," in Lax and Taboada, *Just Above Midtown*, 74.
6. James Nestor, *Breath: The New Science of a Lost Art* (New York: Penguin Random House, 2020).
7. Christina Sharpe, *Ordinary Notes* (New York: Farrar, Straus and Giroux, 2023), 237.

NOTES

1. Johnson, *Modern Art and the Object,* pp. 110, 115.
2. Battcock, *The New Art,* p. 60.
3. John Elderfield, *Morris Louis* (London: Hayward Gallery, June 27-September 1, 1974), p. 10.
4. Robert Doty interview with the artist, September 14, 1971.
5. Donald Miller, "Hanging Loose: An Interview with Sam Gilliam," *Art News* (January, 1973), p. 42.
6. Lucie-Smith, *Late Modern: The Visual Arts Since 1945,* p. 103.
7. Battcock, p. 200-201.
8. Authors' interview with the artist in his studio, August 16, 1977.
9. Authors' interview with the artist, August 17, 1977.
10. Authors' interview with the artist in his studio, August 16, 1977.
11. Hunter, *American Art of the 20th Century,* p. 380.
12. Artist's letter to the authors, August 23, 1977.
13. Frederick Eversley, *Frederick Eversley* (Santa Barbara: Santa Barbara Museum of Art), no page.
14. Authors' interview with the artist, August 17, 1977.
15. Hunter, p. 265.
16. Lippard, *Pop Art,* p. 85-86.
17. *Ibid,* p. 95.
18. Hunter, p. 354.
19. Battcock, *Minimal Art: A Critical Anthology,* p. 305.
20. *Ibid.,* p. 205.
21. *Ibid.,* p. 285.
22. See illustrations: *Marvin Brown* (Melbourne: The Victorian College of the Arts, August 11-September 2, 1977).
23. Walker, *Art Since Pop,* p. 34.
24. Hunter, p. 389.
25. In discussion with the artist during August-September, 1977.
26. Walker, p. 54.
27. Meyer, *Conceptual Art,* p. 202.
28. Artist's letter to the authors, August 29, 1977.
29. See Taylor Branch, "New Frontiers in American Philosophy," *New York Times Magazine* (August 14, 1977), p. 13.
30. In discussion with the artist, during August-September, 1977.
31. Ibid.
32. John Perreault, "On Art," *Soho Weekly News* (March 24-30, 1977).
33. Statement by the artist on occasion of her exhibition at Just Above Midtown, March, 1977.
34. Written statement by the artist, 1976-1977.
35. Ibid.
36. Ibid.
37. Ibid.
38. Ibid.
39. Authors' interview with the artist, August 19, 1977.
40. Authors' interview with the artist, August 25, 1977.
41. Ibid.
42. Houston Conwill, "Interview with Betye Saar," *Black Art Quarterly* (to be published Winter, 1978).
43. Channing D. Johnson, "Betye Saar's 'Hoodoo' World of Art," *Essence* (March, 1975), p. 85.
44. Cindi Nemser, "Conversations with Betye Saar," *The Feminist Art Journal* (Winter 1975-1976), p. 20.
45. Authors' interview with the artist, August 17, 1977.
46. Written statement of the artist, 1976.
47. *Ibid.*
48. *Ibid.*
49. *Ibid.*
50. Authors' interview with the artist during August-September, 1977.
51. Written statement of the artist, 1976.
52. Barry Craig, "A Ritual Experience," *Art Week* (October 25, 1975).
53. Lawrence Alloway, "Art," *The Nation* (November 8, 1975), p. 477.
54. Authors' interview with the artist, August 17, 1977.
55. Statement of the artist, August, 1977.
56. Ibid.
57. Authors' interview with the artist in his studio, August 15, 1977.
58. Ibid.
59. Ibid.
60. Hilton Kramer, "Review," *The New York Times* (April 8, 1977).

BIBLIOGRAPHY

BOOKS

Arnason, H. Harvard. *History of Modern Art.* New York: Harry N. Abrams, 1968.

Ashton, Dore. *The New York School.* New York: The Viking Press, 1972.

Battcock, Gregory, ed. *Minimal Art: A Critical Anthology.* New York: E.P. Dutton & Co., 1968.

Battcock, Gregory, ed. *The New Art.* New York: E.P. Dutton & Co., 1966.

Battcock, Gregory, ed. *Super Realism.* New York: E.P. Dutton & Co., 1975.

Bearden, Romare and Henderson, Harry. *6 Black Masters of American Art.* Garden City, New York: Doubleday & Company, Inc., 1972.

Dover, Cedric. *American Negro Art.* New York: New York Graphic Society, 1960.

Fax, Elton C. *17 Black Artists.* New York: Dodd, Mead & Company, 1971.

Gayle, Addison, Jr., ed. *The Black Aesthetic.* Garden City, New York: Doubleday & Company, Inc., 1972.

Gheldzahler, Henry. *American Painting in the Twentieth Century.* New York: The Metropolitan Museum of Art, 1965.

Hunter, Sam and Jacobus, John. *American Art of the 20th Century.* New York: Harry N. Abrams, 1973.

Johnson, Ellen. *Modern Art and the Object.* New York: Harper & Row, 1976.

Kozloff, Max. *Rendering.* New York: Simon & Schuster, 1961.

Lippard, Lucy. *Pop Art.* New York: Praeger World of Art Paperbacks, 1966.

Lucie-Smith, Edward. *Late Modern: The Visual Arts Since 1945.* New York: Frederick A. Praeger, 1967.

Meyers, Ursula. *Conceptual Art.* New York: E.P. Dutton & Co., 1972.

Rodman, Selden. *Conversations with Artists.* New York: Capricorn Books, 1961.

Rose, Barbara, ed. *Readings in American Art Since 1900.* New York: Frederick A. Praeger, 1968.

Rosenberg, Harold. *Art on the Edge.* New York: Macmillan Publishing Co., Inc., 1971.

Rosenberg, Harold. *The De-definition of Art.* New York: Collier Books, 1972.

Rubin, William. *Frank Stella.* New York: The Museum of Modern Art, 1970.

Shapiro, David, ed. *Social Realism: Art As a Weapon.* New York: Frederick Ungar Publishing Co., 1973.

Walker, John A. *Art Since Pop.* London, England: Thames & Hudson, 1975.

CATALOGUES

Afro-American Artists. The School of the Museum of Fine Arts, Boston, Massachusetts, May 19-June 23, 1970.

Alma W. Thomas. Howard University Gallery of Art, Washington, D.C., October 22-November 14, 1975.

Alma W. Thomas. Martha Jackson Gallery, New York, October 23-November 17, 1976.

Brown, Milton. *Jacob Lawrence.* Whitney Museum of American Art, New York, May 16-July 7, 1974.

Contemporary Art: 1942-1972. Albright-Knox Art Gallery collection catalogue, New York, 1972.

Craig, Barry. *Recent Works by Houston Conwill.* The Gallery, Los Angeles, May, 1976.

Driskill, David C. *Two Centuries of Black American Art.* New York: Alfred A. Knopf, 1976.

Elderfield, John. *Morris Louis.* Hayward Gallery, London, June 27-September 1, 1974.

Feinberg, Joy. *Raymond Saunders: Recent Work.* University Art Museum, Berkeley, California, January 6-February 22, 1976.

5 + 1. State University of New York at Stony Brook, Stony Brook, New York, October 16-November 8, 1969.

Frank Bowling. Center for Inter-American Relations, New York, November 20, 1973-January 13, 1974.

Frank Bowling: Selected Paintings 1967-1977. The Acme Gallery, London, April 15-May 7, 1977.

Frederick Eversley. Santa Barbara Museum of Art, Santa Barbara, April 30-May, 1976.

Hopps, Walter. *John E. Dowell, Jr.: Recent Drawings and Paintings.* Lunn Gallery, Washington, D.C., September 18-October 10, 1973.

Hopps, Walter. *Sam Gilliam: Paintings and Works on Paper.* The J.B. Speed Art Museum, Louisville, Kentucky, January 12-February 8, 1976.

Kainen, Jacob. *John E. Dowell, Jr.: Prints and Drawings.* The Corcoran Gallery of Art, Washington, D.C., March 26-May 2, 1971.

Legg, Alicia. *American Art Since 1945.* New York: The Museum of Modern Art, 1975 (for travelling exhibition).

Marvin Brown. The Victorian College of the Arts, Melbourne, Australia, August 11-September 2, 1977.

Robins, Corinne. *Drawing Now.* Soho Center for Visual Artists, New York, June 3-June 26, 1976.

Serwer, Jacqueline Days. *Gilliam/Edwards/Williams: Extensions.* The Wadsworth Atheneum, Hartford, February 6-May 14, 1974.

Solomon, Elke and Robert. *John E. Dowell, Jr.: Rome 1971-74.* Temple Abroad, Tyler School of Art in Rome, Rome, February 19-April 1, 1974.

Tucker, Marcia. *Betye Saar.* Whitney Museum of American Art, New York, March 20-April 20, 1975.

MAGAZINES AND NEWSPAPER ARTICLES

Adrian, Dennis. "Paintings to Muse On, and Music to Paint By," *Chicago Daily News,* March 6-7, 1976.

Alloway, Lawrence. "Art," *The Nation,* November 8, 1975. p. 477.

Ashton, Dore. "Young Abstract Painters Right On!," *Arts Magazine,* February, 1970, p. 31 + .

Baker, Kenneth. "Reviews," *Artforum,* June, 1972, p. 86.

"The Black Artist: A Symposium with Romare Bearden, Sam Gilliam, Richard Hunt, Jacob Lawrence, Tom Lloyd, William T. Williams, Hale Woodruff," *The Metropolitan Museum of Art Bulletin,* January, 1969, p. 243 + .

Bloom, Janet, "5 + 1," *Arts Magazine,* December-January, 1970-71, p. 56.

Bowling, Frank. "Discussion on Black Art, Part I," *Arts Magazine,* April, 1969, p. 16 + .

Bowling, Frank. "Discussion on Black Art, Part II," *Arts Magazine,* May, 1969, p. 20 + .

Branch, Taylor. "New Frontiers in American Philosophy," *The New York Times Magazine,* August 14, 1977, p. 12 + .

Conwill, Houston. "Interview with Betye Saar," *Black Art Quarterly,* to be published Winter, 1978.

Conwill, Houston. "Nine Artists Show in 'Festival in Black'," *Art Week,* August 13, 1977.

Craig, Barry. "A Ritual Experience," *Art Week,* October 25, 1975.

Donohoe, Victoria. "Art," *The Philadelphia Inquirer,* May 6, 1977.

Forman, Nessa. "There's a Flaw in John Dowell's Oyster," *The Sunday Bulletin,* May 1, 1977.

Hultgren, Ann. "Reviews," *The New Art Examiner,* June, 1976.

Johnson, Channing D. "Betye Saar's 'Hoodoo' World of Art," *Essence,* March, 1975, p. 84 + .

Kramer, Hilton. "Review," *The New York Times,* April 8, 1977.

Lewis, Jo Ann. "Squiggles that Dance in Space," *Washington Star News,* September 21, 1973.

Miller, Donald. "Hanging Loose: An Interview with Sam Gilliam," *Art News,* January, 1973, p. 42 + .

Miller, Donald. "Three-Woman Art Show," *Pittsburgh Post Gazette,* May 13, 1970.

Nemser, Cindi. "Conversation with Betye Saar," *The Feminist Art Journal,* Winter, 1975-1976.

Perreault, John. "On Art," *Soho Weekly News,* March 24-30, 1977.

Perreault, John. "Review," *Soho Weekly News,* April 21, 1977, p. 19.

Ratcliff, Carter. "New York," *Art International,* April, 1970, p. 67 + .

Ratcliff, Carter. "The Paint Thickens," *Artforum,* Summer, 1976, p. 46.

Robins, Corinne. "Edward Clark: Push-Broom and Canvas," *Art International,* October, 1973, P. 36 + .

Rose, Barbara. "Black Art in America," *Art in America.* September-October, 1970, p. 54 + .

Seldis, Henry J. "Optical Magic Turns Us Inward as We Look Out," *The Los Angeles Times,* May 23, 1976, p. 76 + .

Sims, Lowery. "Noah Jemison," *Arts Magazine,* January, 1977, p. 14.

Webster, Daniel. "He Puts Art into His Music," *The Philadelphia Inquirer,* April 7, 1976, p. 3-C.

COLOR PLATES

1. ED CLARK. *Integrated Oval, I.* 1972. Acrylic on canvas, 114 × 175½ inches. Collection of John Slimak, Chicago, Ill. Courtesy of the Artist.
2. SUZANNE JACKSON. *Splash.* 1976. Acrylic on canvas, 80 × 80 inches. Collection of Ankrum Gallery, Los Angeles.
3. FRANK BOWLING. *Valley.* 1977. Acrylic on canvas, 77 × 33 inches. Courtesy of Tibor de Nagy Gallery, New York.
4. AL LOVING. *Untitled.* 1977. Mixed media on canvas, 60 × 60 inches. Collection of Fischbach Gallery, New York. Courtesy of the Artist.
5. WILLIAM T. WILLIAMS. *Sophie Jackson, L.A.M.F.* 1969. Acrylic on canvas, 60 × 84 inches. Courtesy of the Artist.
6. SHARON SUTTON. *Fading of the Fabulous Olden Lady.* 1976. Colored drawing, 21½ × 21½ inches. Courtesy of the Artist.
7. MEL EDWARDS. *Try, Try.* 1973. Painted steel and chain. Courtesy of the Artist.
8. JOHN DOWELL. *To Dance Yesterday's Dreams.* 1977. Acrylic on canvas, 5 × 7 feet. Courtesy of the Artist.
9. DAVID HAMMONS. *Gray Skies Over Harlem.* 1977. Hair, wire, eggs, roaches, tea bags and feathers. Courtesy of Just Above Midtown Gallery, New York.
10. WENDY WARD EHLERS. *Traces.* 1974/75. Wood and dryer lint. Courtesy of the Artist.
11. HOUSTON CONWILL. *Juju Installation.* 1977. Gut bucket, ceremonial stool, rocks and sand. Courtesy of the Artist.
12. HOWARDENA PINDELL. *Untitled #83.* 1977. Paper, thread, board, 12½ × 18 inches. Courtesy of Just Above Midtown Gallery, New York.
13. BANERJEE. *Fern Horns Hundred.* 1976. Origami construction of painted blue print paper, fumage, oil-stain, charcoal, lead and colored pencil with latex, 68 × 48 inches. Courtesy of Just Above Midtown Gallery, New York.
14. NOAH JEMISON. *The Mythological Allegory of the Real Chumpy-Do.* 1977. Wax, sewn canvas and pigment. Courtesy of Just Above Midtown Gallery, New York.
15. NOAH JEMISON. *Divorce.* 1977. Wax and pigment, 4 × 6 feet. Courtesy of Just Above Midtown Gallery, New York.
16. RANDY WILLIAMS. *Twenty-Three Years of Black American Art.* 1977. Wood, book, shoe shine stand, album and washboard. Courtesy of Just Above Midtown Gallery, New York.

LIST OF ILLUSTRATIONS

1. ED CLARK. *Black and White Drawings. 1970.* Ink and pastel on paper, 30 × 40 inches. Courtesy of the Artist. *Ill. p. 15*
2. SUZANNE JACKSON. *Witches, Bitches and Loons. 1972.* Acrylic wash, 54 × 72 inches. Collection of D.R. Gould and Associates, Los Angeles. Courtesy of Ankrum Gallery, Los Angeles. *Ill. p. 17*
3. FRANK BOWLING. *Cathedral. 1975.* Acrylic on canvas, 79 × 47 inches. Collection of F.B. Shaw T & N. Courtesy of Tibor de Nagy Gallery, New York. *Ill. p. 18*
4. SAM GILLIAM. *Untitled. 1971.* Dye stain, 20¼ × 25½ inches. Collection of The Museum Of Modern Art, New York. Acquired with matching funds from The Lily Auchincloss Foundation and The National Endowment For The Arts. *Ill. p. 19*
5. JAMES LITTLE. *Dark Cloud Passing Before the Sun. 1977.* Ink on paper, 22 × 30 inches. Courtesy of the Artist. *Ill. p. 20*
6. JAMES LITTLE. *Overtures. 1977.* Ink on paper, 22 × 30 inches. Courtesy of the Artist. *Ill. p. 20*
7. AL LOVING. *Untitled.* Courtesy of the Studio Museum In Harlem, New York. *Ill. p. 22*
8. WILLIAM T. WILLIAMS. *Elbert Jackson, L.A.M.F. Part II. 1969.* Synthetic polymer paint and metallic paint on canvas, 109-7/8 × 115¼ inches. Collection of The Museum Of Modern Art, New York. Gift of Mrs. John R. Jakobson, Carter Burdern and Mr. & Mrs. John R. Purchase. *Ill. p. 23*
9. SHARON SUTTON. *This Box Is Our Box. 1972.* Lithograph, 27 × 27 inches. Courtesy of Just Above Midtown Gallery, New York. *Ill. p. 23*
10. FRED EVERSLEY. *Untitled #9. 1975.* Cast polyester resin, 36 inches × 91.4 cm. Courtesy of Andrew Crispo Gallery, Inc. New York. *Ill. p. 24*
11. MEL EDWARDS. *The Fourth Circle. 1966.* Painted steel. Courtesy of the Artist. *Ill. p. 25*
12. RAYMOND SAUNDERS. *Dr. Jesus. 1969.* Oil, 45 × 58 inches. Courtesy of Terry Dintenfass, Inc., New York. *Ill. p. 30*
13. RAYMOND SAUNDERS. *1,2,3,4,5. 1974.* Mixed media, 83½ × 68½ inches. Courtesy of Terry Dintenfass Gallery, Inc. New York. *Ill. p. 31*
14. MANUAL HUGHES. *Thrice Light. 1976.* Pastel on paper, 25½ × 19-5/8 inches. Courtesy of the Artist. *Ill. p. 33*
15. JOHN DOWELL. *L.P.W.S. (Lines Played With Soul). 1976.* Serigraph. Courtesy of the Artist. *Ill. p. 35*
16. DAVID HAMMONS. *Black Boy's Window. (detail). 1968.* Mixed media, 27¾ × 35¾ inches. Collection of Dale Davis. Courtesy of Just Above Midtown Gallery, New York. *Ill. p. 37*
17. DAVID HAMMONS. *Black Boy's Window. 1968.* Mixed Media, 27¾ × 35¾ inches. Collection of Dale Davis. Courtesy of Just Above Midtown Gallery, New York. *Ill. p. 38*
18. DAVID HAMMONS. *Close Your Eyes and See Black. 1970.* Body print, 26 × 27 inches. Courtesy of Just Above Midtown Gallery, New York. *Ill. p. 42*
19. DAVID HAMMONS. *Laughing Magic. 1973.* Spade, ties, and chains. Collection of Stevie Wonder. Courtesy of Just Above Midtown Gallery, New York. *Ill. p. 44*
20. DAVID HAMMONS. *Ragged Spirits. 1974.* Body print, 20 × 26 inches. Courtesy of Just Above Midtown Gallery, New York. *Ill. p. 42*
21. DAVID HAMMONS. *Untitled. 1976/77.* Bag, grease, hair and sparkles. Courtesy of Just Above Midtown Gallery, New York. *Ill. p. 45*
22. DAVID HAMMONS. *Untitled. 1976.* Human hair. Courtesy of Just Above Midtown Gallery, New York. *Ill. p. 46*
23. DAVID HAMMONS. *Untitled. 1977.* Human hair and wire. Courtesy of Just Above Midtown Gallery, New York. *Ill. p. 47*
24. DAVID HAMMONS. *Untitled. 1977.* Hair and wire. Courtesy of Just Above Midtown Gallery, New York. *Ill. p. 48*
25. SENGA NENGUDI. *Inside/Outside. 1977.* Nylon mesh, rubber and foam, 5 × 2 feet. Courtesy of Just Above Midtown Gallery, New York. *Ill. p. 49*
26. SENGA NENGUDI. *Chant. 1977.* Nylon mesh and metal pins, 5 × 1 feet. Collection of Barbara Mitchell. Courtesy of Just Above Midtown, New York. *Ill. p. 51*
27. SENGA NENGUDI. *R.S.V.P. XIII. 1977.* Nylon mesh and sand, 5 × 12 feet. Courtesy of Just Above Midtown Gallery, New York. *Ill. p. 51*
28. SENGA NENGUDI. *Swing Low. 1977.* Nylon mesh and sand, 3½ × 4 × 5½ feet. Courtesy of Just Above Midtown Gallery, New York. *Ill. p. 52*
29. SENGA NENGUDI. *Insides Out. 1977.* Nylon mesh and sand, 1 × 10 feet. Courtesy of Just Above Midtown Gallery, New York. *Ill. p. 52*
30. SENGA NENGUDI. *I. 1977.* Nylon mesh and sand, installation piece. Courtesy of Just Above Midtown Gallery, New York. *Ill. p. 53*
31. SENGA NENGUDI. *I. 1977.* Nylon mesh and sand, Installation piece. Courtesy of Just Above Midtown Gallery, New York. *Ill. p. 10*
32. SENGA NENGUDI. *Internal I. 1977.* Nylon mesh, 12 × 6 × 5 feet. Courtesy of Just Above Midtown Gallery, New York. *Ill. p. 54*
33. SENGA NENGUDI. *Internal II. 1977.* Nylon mesh, 12 × 6 × 5 feet. Courtesy of Just Above Midtown, New York. *Ill. p. 55*
34. SUSAN FITZSIMMONS. *Water—Summer. 1977.* Wood, lucite and remains. Courtesy of Just Above Midtown Gallery, New York. *Ill. p. 56*
35. SUSAN FITZSIMMONS. *Water—Fall. 1977.* Lucite, wood and remains. Courtesy of Just Above Midtown Gallery, New York. *Ill. p. 56*
36. SUSAN FITZSIMMONS. *Stick-Caught Cube. 1977.* Wood and lucite. Courtesy of Just Above Midtown Gallery, New York. *Ill. p. 57*
37. GINI HAMILTON. *Love Letter. 1977.* Paper, muslin, painted canvas, string and metal, 25 × 20½ inches. Courtesy of the Artist. *Ill. p. 58*
38. GINI HAMILTON. *Option: Continuance. 1977.* Steel, cotton and string. Courtesy of the Artist. *Ill. p. 59*
39. WENDY EHLERS. *Three Inches Equals One Week of Laundry. 1974.* Dryer lint. Courtesy of the Artist. *Ill. p. 61*
40. WENDY EHLERS. *Feather Floor Piece. 1977.* Feathers and wood. Courtesy of the Artist. *Ill. p. 61*
41. BETYE SAAR. *Last Dance. 1975.* Mixed media, 12 × 14¼ inches. Courtesy of Monique Knowlton Gallery, New York. *Ill. p. 63*
42. BETYE SAAR. *Ohne Hast, Ohne Rast. 1976.* Mixed media, 14 × 17 × ¾ inches. Courtesy of Monique Knowlton Gallery, New York. *Ill. p. 63*
43. HOUSTON CONWILL. *Edison Tale (detail). 1976/77.* Petrigraph. Courtesy of the Artist. *Ill. p. 64*
44. DONNA BYARS. *Oracle Stone's Grove. 1977.* Trees, chair and stones. 6 × 5 × 5 feet. Courtesy of the Artist. *Ill. p. 65*
45. DONNA BYARS. *Rabbit Pen—A Reclamation. 1976.* Pen, bandaged rabbit, clay pots. 7 × 5½ × 7-3/8 inches. Courtesy of the Artist. *Ill. p. 65*
46. DONNA BYARS. *Vested Relic. 1977.* Slatted cage, fabric, shell and silver wing, 8 × 7 × 4¾ inches. Courtesy of the Artist. *Ill. p. 66*
47. DONNA BYARS. *The Secret. 1977.* Cloth and wood, 58 × 18 × 29 inches. Courtesy of the Artist. *Ill. p. 66*
48. HOWARDENA PINDELL. *Untitled #4. 1973.* Pen and ink on paper, mounted on graph paper, 25-3/8 × 18¾ inches. Collection of The

Museum Of Modern Art, New York. Gift of Mrs. John D. Rockefeller. *Ill. p. 68*

49. HOWARDENA PINDELL. *Untitled #88. 1977.* Acrylic, gouache, watercolor and thread, 13 × 14½ inches. Courtesy of the Artist. *Ill. p. 69*
50. HOWARDENA PINDELL. *Video Drawing: Swimming Series. 1976.* Color photograph, 5 × 7 inches. Courtesy of the Artist. *Ill. p. 70*
51. BANERJEE. *Characterscape. 1965.* Monotype of wax, dry leaves, hair, and hair net on paper, 36 × 24 inches. Courtesy of the Artist. *Ill. p. 71*
52. BANERJEE. *Diagonal Origamis #2. 1971.* 60 × 48 inches. Courtesy of the Artist. *Ill. p. 71*
53. BANERJEE. *Ram Horn in Foliage. 1976.* Origami collage of inked and painted rice paper, fumage, watercolor and pencil on paper 22½ × 28 inches. Courtesy of the Artist. *Ill. p. 6*
54. NOAH JEMISON. *Walking Through The Universe (Happy As A Pig In Shit). 1977.* Wax, sewn canvas and pigment, 3 × 4 feet. Courtesy of Just Above Midtown Gallery, New York. *Ill. p. 73*
55. RANDY WILLIAMS. *Untitled October #1. 1977.* Bag, string, canvas, acrylic and graphite on paper. 24 × 30 inches. Courtesy of Just Above Midtown Gallery, New York. *Ill. p. 75*
56. RANDY WILLIAMS. *Merchants and Masterpieces. 1977.* Wood, books, frames, paint brush, rope and ruler, 47½ × 35 × 7 inches. Courtesy of Just Above Midtown Gallery, New York. *Ill. p. 76*
57. RANDY WILLIAMS. *L'Art Abstract. 1977.* Book, wood and acrylic wash, 23½ × 39½ inches. Courtesy of Just Above Midtown Gallery, New York. *Ill. p. 2*
58. RANDY WILLIAMS. *Homage To The Edge Of A Corner. 1977.* Wood, wire, razor blades, installation piece. Courtesy of Just Above Midtown Gallery, New York. *Ill. p. 78*

PHOTO CREDITS

Adam Avila Photography, cover; Lee Abramson, 10; Geva-inkeri, 18; Suzanne Kaufman, 20; Frank Stewart, 22; Frank Stewart, 23; Walter Rosenblum, 30; Geoffrey Clements, 31; Kate Keller, 33; Bruce W. Talamon, 38; Frank J. Thomas, 42; Frank J. Thomas, 44; Lee Abramson, 53; Lesley Saar, 63; Douglas Parker, 64; Maude Boltz, 65; Maude Boltz, 66.

INDEX

A Abstract Expressionism, 13, 14, 15, 19, 20, 27, 39, 69; Andre, Carl, 32; Anti-Form, 31.

B Banerjee, 69, 70, 71, 72; Body prints, 40, 41; Bowling, Frank, 16, 17; Brown, Marvin, 29; Byars, Donna, 64, 65, 66.

C Cezanne, Paul, 13; Clark, Ed, 14; Close, Chuck, 29; Color-field Art, 16; Conceptual Art, 33; Contextural Art, 39, 40, 41, 42, 43, 45, 46, 47, 48, 50, 53, 60, 62, 63, 64, 65, 66, 67, 69, 70, 71, 72, 73, 74, 75, 77, 78; Conwill, Houston, 63, 64; Cubism, 13.

D Dada, 13, 26, 27, 39, 40, 78; DeKooning, Willem, 32, 66; Dine, Jim, 27; Discards, 40, 53, 60, 75; Dowell, John, 32, 33, 75; Duchamp, Marcel, 13, 33, 39, 40, 41.

E Earthworks, 32; Edwards, Mel, 23, 26; Ehlers, Wendy Ward, 60; Encaustic, 72; Eversley, Fred, 23.

F Federal Art Project, 14; Fitzsimmons, Susan, 47, 48, 50, 63; Frankenthaler, Helen, 16; Fumage, 40, 70, 71, 72.

G Gilliam, Sam, 18, 63.

H Hair works, 40, 42, 43; Hamilton, Gini, 50, 53, 60; Hammons, David, 39, 40, 41, 42, 43, 63; Hard-edged Art, 20, 21, 22, 74; Heizer, Michael, 32; Hughes, Manuel, 29, 31.

I Impressionism, 13.

J Jackson, Suzanne, 16; Jemison, Noah, 72, 73, 74; Jewish Museum, 28; John Weber Gallery, 29; Johns, Jasper, 26, 40; Judd, Donald, 28, 29; Junk Art, 26.

K Kinetic Art, 23; Klein, Yves, 40; Kline, Franz, 14, 32.

L LeWitt, Sol, 29; Lichtenstein, Roy, 27; Lint, 60; Little, James, 19; Long, Richard, 32; Louis, Morris, 16, 20; Loving, Al, 20, 21.

M Marasol, 40; Minimal Art, 28, 31, 32, 33; Modal logic, 39; Morris, Robert, 31, 32; The Museum of Modern Art, 21.

N Nengudi, Senga, 43, 45, 46, 47, 50, 53; Neo-Dada, 26, 27; New Realism, 29; Newman, Barnett, 19; Noland, Kenneth, 20; Nylong works, 43, 45, 46, 47.

O Oldenburg, Claes, 27; Op Art, 21, 22, 28, 74; Origami, 70, 71, 72.

P Pearlstein, Philip, 29; Petrigraph, 64; Pindell, Howardena, 66, 67, 69; Piper, Adrian, 33; Pollock, Jackson, 14, 15, 16; Poons, Larry, 22, 66; Process Art, 31, 32, 33.

R Rauschenberg, Robert, 26; Reinhardt, Ad, 19; Ready-mades, 40, 53; Remains, 39, 64; Riley, Bridget, 22; Rivers, Larry, 27; Rothko, Mark, 14.

S Saar, Betye, 62, 63; Saunders, Raymond, 27, 28; Segal, George, 40; Shaped canvas, 21; Siqueiros, David Alfaro, 14; Smithson, Robert, 32; Smokehouse Group, 21; Soak-stain process, 16, 17, 18; Stella, Frank, 20, 21; Super Realism, 29; Surrealism, 13, 27, 39; Sutton, Sharon, 22.

T Template, 66, 67; Thomas, Alma, 17, 18.

V Video Drawings, 69.

W Warhol, Andy, 27; Whitney Museum of American Art, 20, 26; Williams, Randy, 40, 74, 75, 77, 78; Williams, William T., 21.

CREDITS

Characterscape, *Diagonal Origamis #2, Fern Horns in Hundred*, and *Ram Horn in Foliage* by Bimal Banerjee © 2024 Bimal Banerjee / Artists Rights Society (ARS), New York.

Cathedral and *Valley* by Frank Bowling © 2024 Frank Bowling. All Rights Reserved / Artists Rights Society (ARS), New York / DACS, London.

Black and White Drawings and *Integrated Oval I* by Ed Clark
© 2024 The Estate of Ed Clark.

L.P.W.S. (Lines Played With Soul) and *To Dance Yesterday's Dreams*
by John Dowell © 2024 John Dowell.

The Fourth Circle and *Try, Try* by Melvin Edwards © 2024 Melvin Edwards / Artists Rights Society (ARS), New York. Courtesy Alexander Gray Associates, New York; Stephen Friedman Gallery, London.

Untitled #9 by Fred Eversley © 2024 Fred Eversley.
Courtesy of David Kordansky Gallery.

Stick-Caught Cube, *Water—Fall,* and *Water—Summer* by Susan Fitzsimmons
© 2024 Susan Fitzsimmons.

Untitled by Sam Gilliam © 2024 Sam Gilliam / Artists Rights Society (ARS), New York.

Black Boy's Window, *Close your Eyes and See Black*, *Gray Skies Over Harlem*, *Laughing Magic*, *Ragged Spirits*, *Untitled* (1976), *Untitled* (1976/77), *Untitled* (1977), and *Untitled* (1977) by David Hammons
© 2024 David Hammons / Artists Rights Society (ARS), New York.

Dark Cloud Passing Before the Sun and *Overtures* by James Little
© 2024 James Little. Courtesy of Petzel Gallery.

Untitled by Al Loving © 2024 Estate of Al Loving.
Courtesy of the Estate of Al Loving and Garth Greenan Gallery, New York.

Chant, *Costume Study for Mesh Mirage*, *I*, *Insides Out*, *Inside/Outside*, *Internal I*, *Internal II*, *R.S.V.P. XIII*, and *Swing Low* by Senga Nengudi
© Senga Nengudi. Courtesy of the artist and Thomas Erben Gallery, New York.

Untitled #4, *Untitled #83*, *Untitled #88*, and *Video Drawing: Swimming Series*
by Howardena Pindell © 2024 Howardena Pindell.
Courtesy of the artist and Garth Greenan Gallery, New York.

Last Dance and *Ohne Hast, Ohne, Rast* by Betye Saar © 2024 Betye Saar.
Courtesy of the artist and Roberts Projects, Los Angeles, CA.

Contextures

ISBN: 979-8-9876249-2-0

"Contextures: An Afterword"

Contextures was originally published in 1978 by Just Above Midtown gallery. This new edition is published in facsimile form, along with a new afterword, by Pacific and Primary Information.

Editors (1978): Linda Goode Bryant and Marcy S. Philips
Managing Editors (2024): Elizabeth Karp-Evans and James Hoff
Designer (2024): Pacific

Pacific
70 Flushing Avenue
Brooklyn, NY 11205
www.pacificpacific.pub

Primary Information
232 Third Street, #A113
Brooklyn, NY 11215
www.primaryinformation.org

Printed by Grafiche Veneziane

Special thanks to Linda Goode Bryant, Alexander Gray Associates, Garth Greenan Gallery, Thomas Erben Gallery, Hauser & Wirth, David Kordansky Gallery, Thomas (T.) Jean Lax, Petzel Gallery, Roberts Projects, Barry Rosen, and Michael Rosenfeld Gallery.

Primary Information is a 501(c)(3) non-profit organization founded in 2006 to publish artists' books and writings. The organization's programming advances the often-intertwined relationship between artists' books and arts activism, creating a platform for historically marginalized artistic communities and practices. Primary Information receives generous support through grants from the Michael Asher Foundation, Galerie Buchholz, the Patrick and Aimee Butler Family Foundation, The Cowles Charitable Trust, Empty Gallery, The Ford Foundation, The Fox Aarons Foundation, the Helen Frankenthaler Foundation, Furthermore: a program of the J. M. Kaplan Fund, the Graham Foundation for Advanced Studies in the Fine Arts, Greene Naftali, the Greenwich Collection Ltd, the John W. and Clara C. Higgins Foundation, Metabolic Studio, the National Endowment for the Arts, the New York City Department of Cultural Affairs in partnership with the City Council, the New York State Council on the Arts with the support of the Office of the Governor and the New York State Legislature, the Orbit Fund, the Stichting Egress Foundation, VIA Art Fund, The Jacques Louis Vidal Charitable Fund, The Andy Warhol Foundation for the Visual Arts, the Wilhelm Family Foundation, and individuals worldwide. Primary Information receives support from the Arison Arts Foundation, the Willem de Kooning Foundation, the Marian Goodman Foundation, the Henry Luce Foundation, and Teiger Foundation through the Coalition of Small Arts NYC.